A beautiful book exploring the role, fate, and possibilities of gentleness in life. Doctor Barnea-Astrog draws from psychoanalysis and Buddhism and a rich reservoir of resources that play a role in our makeup. She discusses difficulties we face and supports us in our quest for opening to the call of existence, its mysteries and hopes. A long-overdue caring, thoughtful, and detailed study of the importance of gentleness, its challenges and gifts.

Michael Eigen, *The Challenge of Being Human*

Barnea-Astrog's choice to study "gentleness" as a phenomenon and consider it in a way hitherto unattempted in psychoanalysis is astounding. Her book offers a rich, profound yet simple and accessible lexicon of psychoanalytic and Buddhist insights and their interrelations, which enables us to understand gentleness as an existential substrate and avenue to a unique experience of being in the world. The author's personal manner of writing, interspersed with clinical vignettes and illustrations from both western and eastern wisdom, allows for an exciting and instructive, intimate and dreaming associative reading experience. In tumultuous and violent times, this book not only illuminates but also holds out the relief of gentleness.

Merav Roth, PhD, Psychoanalyst, Chair of Klein studies and PhD interdisciplinary unit for psychoanalysis in Tel Aviv University, Author of *Reading the Reader – A Psychoanalytic Perspective.*

In this book Michal Barnea-Astrog beautifully describes the experience of gentleness that some of us carry throughout the life cycle. If you have sensed and learned to protect yourself from the too-much-ness of life, you will find yourself in this book. With skill and sensitivity, Barnea-Astrog offers a way to understand and appreciate this gentle nature and the many developmental challenges that accompany it. Using psychoanalytic theory and Buddhist spiritual teachings, she offers the reader a rare glimpse into a way of being that can be supported and nurtured in family systems, communities, and intimate relationships of all kinds. This is a timely book that encourages us all to find our gentleness within and offer it to a world in need of an ethics informed by a tender and open heart.

Pilar Jennings, PhD, psychoanalyst, lecturer, and author of
To Heal a Wounded Heart

Psychoanalytic and Buddhist Reflections on Gentleness

Inspired by Buddhist teachings and psychoanalytic thought, this book explores gentleness as a way of being and a developmental achievement. It offers reflections on the unique position of "gentle people", as well as certain gentle layers of the psyche in general, as they meet the world. Examining the perceptual-sensory-conscious discrepancy that often exists between a gentle person and their surroundings, it follows the intricate relationship between sensitivity and fear, the need for self-holding, and the possibility of letting go.

Incorporating theoretical investigation, clinical vignettes, and personal contemplation, the book looks into those states of mind and qualities of attention that may compose a favorable environment, internal and interpersonal, where gentleness can be delicately held. There, it is suggested, gentleness may gradually shed the fragility, confusion, and destructiveness that often get entangled with it and serve as a valuable recourse.

Offering a unique perspective on a topic rarely discussed, the book has broad appeal for both students and practitioners of psychoanalysis and psychotherapy, as well as Buddhist practitioners and scholars.

Michal Barnea-Astrog, PhD, is a researcher of psychoanalysis and Buddhism, a senior Hakomi trainer, and a therapist in private practice. She teaches at the East Asian Studies Department at Tel Aviv University and is the founder and head of the Three-Year Hakomi Training in Israel. She is the author of *Carved by Experience: Vipassana, Psychoanalysis, and the Mind Investigating Itself*.

Psychoanalytic and Buddhist Reflections on Gentleness

Sensitivity, Fear, and the Drive Towards Truth

Michal Barnea-Astrog

Routledge
Taylor & Francis Group
LONDON AND NEW YORK

First published 2019
by Routledge
2 Park Square, Milton Park, Abingdon, Oxon OX14 4RN

and by Routledge
52 Vanderbilt Avenue, New York, NY 10017

*Routledge is an imprint of the Taylor & Francis Group, an informa
business*

© 2019 Michal Barnea-Astrog

British Library Cataloguing-in-Publication Data
A catalogue record for this book is available from the
British Library

Library of Congress Cataloging-in-Publication Data
Names: Barnea-Astrog, Michal, author.
Title: Psychoanalytic and buddhist reflections on gentleness :
    sensitivity, fear and the drive towards truth / Michal
    Barnea-Astrog.
Description: 1 Edition. | New York : Routledge, 2019. | Includes
    bibliographical references and index.
Identifiers: LCCN 2018050603 | ISBN 9781138371187 (hardback :
    alk. paper) | ISBN 9781138371194 (pbk. : alk. paper) | ISBN
    9780429427732 (eBook)
Subjects: LCSH: Courtesy. | Psychoanalysis. | Buddhism.
Classification: LCC BJ1533.C9 B38 2019 | DDC 177/.1—dc23
LC record available at https://lccn.loc.gov/2018050603

ISBN: 978-1-138-37118-7 (hbk)
ISBN: 978-1-138-37119-4 (pbk)
ISBN: 978-0-429-42773-2 (ebk)

Typeset in Times New Roman
by Apex CoVantage, LLC.

To my beloved Talya and Alona
and to all gentle beings
who take shelter in truth
in this world of mind and matter

Contents

Acknowledgments

Thanks to Tamar Apel, Eilona Ariel, Rony Ben-Ziony, Itai Breuer, Alex Cherniak, Paul R. Fleischman, Maya Gur, Anat Maor, Mirjam Hadar Meerschwam, William Hart, Tammy Hershkovitz, Klaus Nothnagel, Ilana Nutkevitch, Esther Pelled, Jacob Raz, Merav Roth, Yorai Sella, and Galit Yaari;

to Yaron, my enabler,

and to Satya Narayan Goenka, who showed me there is room for sensitivity, that it is not doomed to stay forlorn;

who taught me how one may slowly shift from rigidity to flexibility, and from flexibility to dissolution –

to him, to those who taught him, and to those who learned from him, my models of all that is tender and gentle

those unsurpassed fields of goodness.

***

The people who appear in this book gave their full consent. Their personal details were changed to prevent identification.

Abbreviations.

AN – Aṅguttara Nikāya
Dhp – Dhammapada
DN – Dīgha Nikāya
MN – Majjhima Nikāya
SN – Saṃyutta Nikāya
Snp – Suttanipāta
Ud – Udāna
VIS – Vissudhimagga

Chapter 1

On gentleness

From as long as he remembered himself, Ron had known a sense of fragility. His feelings, he sensed, were always close to the surface – a tender tissue that would crack at the merest touch. It wasn't a great asset in his childhood neighborhood: a Tel Aviv quarter largely populated by former army personnel. It might not have been much better elsewhere.

He spent long stretches alone in his room, listening to music and drawing. An odd bird; that was how his father thought of him, sometimes trying to swallow expressions of contempt and puzzlement, and at other times not even trying. His mother was full of good intentions but couldn't quite figure him out, either. She didn't know what to do with his emotions, or rather, what to do with herself around them.

Ron was not socially isolated. He was quite good at fitting in and made sure he did everything as expected. He joined the Boy Scouts, went to summer camp and to parties, and hung out with friends, pretty much doing what they were doing. But deep inside he felt split: He didn't want to seclude himself, but he also didn't really want to be out there, and occasions they handled with ease, almost lightheartedly, he experienced as a struggle.

He was extremely self-conscious – initially, in the way it sometimes happens with children; next, as adolescents can be, and eventually in the manner of young adults. He looked at himself and felt both different and vulnerable. He decided to take action, to adjust himself and toughen up. Going against his natural grain, he forced himself to listen to loud music and watch violent action movies. He started using the local slang, though inside himself, he flinched.

An unconscious part developed in him that tried to take control of the current of stimuli-experience, from the inside out and from the outside in: to put a brake on any sadness or yearning wherever they arose, and to push away – at least a little – whatever threatened to trigger these feelings. He adopted a swallowing movement that appeared at the first signs of excitement, that he repeated so much it almost seemed a tic, and an involuntary tensing of his jaws and stomach, which in time turned into headaches and stomachaches. Although he felt stronger and better able to meet the world, there was also a price to pay. Something in him was outraged at this imposed discord, and it tried to find its own course.

Not a few people move in the world feeling like a delicate being that somehow strayed into a coarse reality. This experience – more or less conscious, more or less overt – is an ongoing undercurrent of their lives. It amounts to an existential condition in whose light, and on whose basis, all the rest is built: their sense of self, their sense of others, and the relations between them. A woman describes her mother as being made out of materials so unlike her own that there wasn't a chance, from the very outset, to be either seen or understood by her. A man who, due to his need for softness and aesthetics, was under more or less constant assault from the physical harshness of his family home. Another whose father's invasiveness and vulgarity, set off against his own sensitivity and gentleness, caused him to move in and out of states of non-existence in order, paradoxically, to be able to be himself.

Some people are born with certain physical and mental characteristics which make them into what I would call gentle people. What exactly it is that turns them into what they are – inborn traits (genes? intra-uterine experience or experiences during birth? circumstances whose roots lie even further back?); the nature of their relations with early significant figures, or other physical and cultural conditions – none of this is what I would want to try to probe and determine. It is clear, however, that a combination of these factors, interweaving, constantly emerging one from another and creating one another, could easily turn into a complex, inextricable knot.

For some years it looked as though following the beaten track worked well for Ron. After graduating from high school, he joined a prestigious intelligence unit in the army. Though headaches and stomachaches persisted, rising and falling, they never called for more attention than some simple allergy tests followed by largely unsuccessful attempts to cut out lactose or gluten. Somehow he managed the first weeks of his military service. He passed through them as if through a fog, aware, but not quite, of his new reality, withdrawing at every opportunity as he hooked up to his music through headphones. Eventually, however, there was no escape and the environment invaded – grey, ugly, coarse. An immature romantic relationship exposed him to intense feelings, and these in turn touched on painful primitive mental layers and reactivated them. The adaptive-hardening envelope was torn.

"I moved through the [military] base and it hurt, every moment. Everything I passed was something that was about to pass away. Every moment a moment of parting. In the mere passage of time there loomed separation. Separation filled each and every moment, insufferable pain".

It wasn't long before this intolerable pain was joined by frequent panic attacks. Stomachaches and headaches moved into the background in the face of these panic attacks, grew insignificant by comparison. It seemed as if Ron had given up his muscular holding, dropped the pretense of toughness. Once or twice a day all of the world's walls would close in on him, the air growing dense. It could overtake him almost anytime, anywhere. Neon lights could trigger an attack, or the way the room looked. Or, completely arbitrarily, so it seemed, with no good reason at all, he would suddenly feel his brain chemistry changing: some substance would start flowing through his body and mind, causing the entire universe to collapse. There was nowhere safe to be. Only when he was on the road was he safe from the nightmare: being in motion kept it at bay. Sometimes, when he passed by a flowering plant, he'd pick a blossom and inhale the smell. He'd close his eyes and for a few brief moments take his fill of the goodness he yearned for so badly. He needed tenderness and beauty. Coarseness and ugliness grated on him.

To be in the world unheld

Life naturally involves suffering. From its very start until the end, we must take our leave from who and what are dear to us and must encounter what we don't wish for. Birth is attended by pain, to be followed, ineluctably, by sickness, old age, and death, physical and mental agonies, grief and distress. That life is given to constant change; that we are given to constant change, and that whoever and whatever we hold dear is given to constant change – this means separation and misery. The process of becoming and decaying is naturally painful (the first noble truth, according to the Buddha). There is a way out of this process, and this way is fully articulated (the third and fourth noble truths); and those who take it watch as release occurs and feel the consequent happiness and relief. But until one has covered the whole length of this path, life will involve some degree of mental pain. In the case of the infant or child, the question is how this pain is treated, how it is held (Winnicott) or contained and digested (Bion). How the minds of the child's first caregivers hold the pain and digest it, and to what extent the infant's young, tender psyche is ready to absorb this holding and digestion, to allow them to alleviate life's impingements, and to gradually offer themselves to the child and become functions of his or her own.

When a baby comes into the world, she needs a holding environment. Her head weighs heavily and her muscles are weak in extra-uterine gravity. While there are some few things she is already competent enough to do for herself, she is pretty much helpless. I assume that even while still in the womb, she experienced suffering of various kinds, but there, at least, her body was always held. Now this has ended, and it is only natural that this bodily "drop", in the baby's immature psyche, will connect with a general sense of being dropped – a terrifying non-integration and lostness. Physical slippage has an emotional parallel. Much like the parents may fail to collect and hold the infant's limbs in such a way as to instill a sense of security, they may also not succeed in properly holding the parts of her psyche, the raw affects and experiences, the anxieties and distress, as well as the rest of the baby's gropings and signals. In a similar manner, the infant, whose digestive system – mental as much as physical – is not fully developed, depends on others to process the emotional reality on her behalf. Like a young bird whose mother pre-chews and partly pre-digests his food, the infant must rely on the minds of her parents to function as containers capable of taking in the difficult mental components which she projects, then to process them and return them to her in a usable form, one that she can handle and metabolize, one that is life-giving and allows for growth.

If the infant is not appropriately held and contained (something which depends on its caregivers but also on the infant's own traits), there is a threat of disintegration, and a primitive terror of annihilation and obliteration – lurking in the background anyway – is likely to take root (Klein, 1946). This primitive anxiety, though fundamentally unthinkable, can nevertheless be described through images of an endless fall (Winnicott, 1974) or a seepage or scattering through space where an envelope is missing (Bick, 1968). Against this dread the psyche employs survival behaviors producing a "sensory floor" (Ogden, 2004), or a holding "second skin" (Bick, 1968), or again a sensory "wrapping" (Anzieu, 2016). These are the infant's ways of holding itself in the absence of sufficient external holding. Infants may fix their attention on some sensory object (a lamp on the ceiling, say), get immersed, and thus feel that they are being held. They may tighten their muscles to prevent the personality from pouring out, in fantasy, through physical holes. They can also be engaging in constant movement, which produces a sense of continuity experienced as a holding skin (Symington, 1985). We adults, too, do such things: We stare at the TV by way of a holding sensory object; we tense certain muscles continuously and involuntarily to hold ourselves tight; we make sure there's always music in the background so as to avoid frightening gaps; we take the car and drive for hours, just to be in motion, or we engage in repetitive body movements so as to sense ongoing being (Ogden, 2004). There are mental parallels to all of these modes of holding, all of which reflect the system's resourcefulness, and each carrying its own particular burden. The mind can create them by stubborn adherence to a certain mental object (an emotion, memory, image, idea or thought), or by means of an incessant parade of images and thoughts, or by a mental movement that has a tightening quality and that leaves no gaps in the inner space, clustering mental materials into one solid mass (Barnea-Astrog, 2015).

No infant is wholly inured against life's injuries, no matter how good the holding and containing they received, and even if its inborn features allow for their optimal use. Since the quality of holding and containment is measured in relation to the specific needs of the specific child, certain babies are less likely to experience conditions of sufficient ongoing holding and containment. Their sensitivity makes them liable to absorb their surroundings at a higher resolution, and they find themselves frequently hurt. Their parents might find it hard to gauge the nuances of their experiences, to process them and adjust themselves to a possibly demanding and intensive rhythm; the babies, from their side, are more likely to feel overwhelmed and emotionally dropped. This is why, it seems to me, gentle people tend – though not inevitably – to be carrying a sense of terror. Ron, clearly, was such a person. At this time many tender regions, previously covered by a provisional layer of adjustment, were exposed. Here it was that anxiety broke through, acute and irrepressible.

He was helpless in the face of this anxiety. He wrapped himself in sound, inhaled any beauty that came his way, and rested on the continuity of motion. These, however, were no more than feeble arms, a fragile, fleeting sensory floor, fragments of a home, the merest twigs carried along in a stream, offering themselves limply by way of momentary and unconvincing support.

Cigarette smoke trickling from mouth to throat to lungs. A glass of wine. More music. A slice of cake. Minute, insufficient breaths of air which neither heal nor accumulate.

This moment hurts, intolerably. It is unbearable by itself, but the fact that here-it-is-passing-away is unbearable, too. A sharp pinch at the depths of existence.

Each breath. Every moment. Blunt knives. Loneliness without a name, a gaping abyss.

The mind, Ron noticed, crashes on the past and fantasizes the future, but the present moment it cannot abide. Each moment grates. The distance between this moment and the past, the distance between now and the future, drowns the moment in separation. It makes it agonizing, insufferable. He invented a method, trying to catch his mind and force it to live in the present: Now I eat, he told himself again and again as he was eating. Now I lay down my pen. Now I walk. I walk. (Years later, he will smile at himself, realizing that a similar meditation technique was already invented many centuries ago.) It didn't work for him, hardly scratched the surface, and he gave up on it very soon. (Years later, he will learn why.) He couldn't help himself, and life was urging him to do something to somehow extricate himself. On friends' advice, he sought psychological help.

In a sense, the primitive dread of being dropped and unintegrated is universal. But it doesn't stay with all of us to the same extent. Those who do carry the terror of their original breakdown simultaneously fear and are attracted to it. It is the very essence of essenceless horror, the worst of undreamable nightmares. Yet, in order to be truly close to themselves, in order to be themselves, in order to truly be, they need to make contact with it. There is no way, says Winnicott, to fully experience the original breakdown: it is too horrific, and because there was no one there to experience it when it occurred (in Winnicott's view, the subject was yet to emerge) – one could say it was never really experienced. Still, it can be approached, its very margin; it can be touched and its presence sensed. Indeed, for the sake of recovery, this is exactly what needs to happen (Winnicott, 1974; Kolker, 2009). Ron touched the edges of his original breakdown at that time. He was moving against them, and their sharp ends cut into him. If this painful contact with terror was going to transform into a gate to truth and healing, Ron would have to study it inside himself, to study himself in the light of it, through experience and non-violent awareness, in a setting offering the right inner and outer attention.

His first encounter with such an environment was the room of his psychologist, full of spaces and moments of silence. Her personality, her quiet affection, this peculiar, non-mutual relationship – somehow they did the job. How and why it happened, he didn't understand, but he began to feel lighter. Initially, the therapy gave him a break from his panic attacks, and then it directed itself to subterranean layers – those relatively closer to the surface – of Ron's relational patterns. This was the beginning of a more flexible, less fragile way of being. The process developed further when, some years later, he began practicing Vipassana meditation. In time, his ability to look into himself in a less violent manner, and to better digest whatever he found there, grew. He wound his way among the geological tissues, the rocks and pebbles of his mind – casting about between them, crumbling them, from the coarsest to the subtler. First, he faced the panic attacks, which his meditation practice brought to the fore yet again. When these vanished – and even before that, in the breaks between them – he had the space to work through his more general anxiety, which would rise to the surface of his body-mind, subjecting him to its ebb and flow. Then he addressed the dregs of terror, the remaining components, physical and mental, which by this point had become almost entirely divested of personal identity: nightmarish contents, a hyper-aroused state of the nervous system, and the raw matter, the primary pain of primary separation, the open abyss, the tear around the stomach branched throughout his being.

The gap

A gentle person is born. What happens to his gentleness as it encounters the world? To what extent does reality suit it, and to what extent do they clash? Does it meet with a resonant sensitivity tending towards it, engaging, flexing, stretching, and solidifying as the need arises? To what extent does this gentleness get to live, to serve the person as a soft ground from which contact with both the inside and the outside can be formed?

I have been fortunate enough to come across quite a few gentle people in my everyday life. They may be different from one another – light years away. They may feel lonely or isolated, but gentleness connects them. I spot them easily: in a sense, they're my people. I know their pain and their beauty, and I love them straightaway. One might think of their pain as related to the clash between their gentleness and the nature of their physical and emotional surroundings – human or not human. This collision may be almost constant, an undercurrent right beneath the flow of experience; in other cases it may enter the field of experience and leave it again, conveniently forgotten only to burst in once more. It might be thought of as a type of developmental trauma, the kind that occurs when an emotional pain finds no (human, emotional) place to be held (Epstein, 2013). And the various physical and mental formations produced in these people in response to the collision might be conceived as constructions that allow them to live with it, to survive it, to hold onto their slight-rich psyche. Some people are more gentle, some are less; still, rather than offering a characterization of a certain type, I would prefer to examine gentleness as a way of being, a certain mode of being in this life.

The gap that often attends the experience of gentleness is a gap between different levels of perceptual-sensory-conscious resolution. "What I feel", the gentle girl realizes when facing her mother, "you don't feel. What strikes me so intensely, you can't even see". The gap is painful. Any distance and disparity hurt the tender, immature soul. In this case, the gap between the mother's and child's levels of resolution may lead the former to miss out on important parts of the latter's experiential universe, leaving them neglected, cast in the shade. Occurring at a much more benign point on the line, yet nevertheless a little like neglected orphans who, having learned that the hoped-for response will not come, stop crying – the internal and interpersonal links of one who experiences such a gap are bound to suffer distortion. In the place of inner lucidity and straightforward expression, fog and confusion may flourish, as well as poor, twisted communication. The girl, who might have grown up since, does not quite know what's happening to her or what she needs; or maybe she does know, but this knowing is torture, clashing with what experience has taught her about what can and cannot be had in this world, with what she has learned about what is allowed and acceptable, with what she believes someone else may understand.

Distress and even pathology may compile as a result of incompatibility, heaping further layers of suffering on top of the fundamental pain of discrepancy itself. The most easily understood layers – which are also the most accessible to consciousness – involve the environment's attitude and the subsequent formation of a sense of self. The people surrounding a gentle person may be critical of him, contemptuous, angry; they may not understand, or they may be frustrated with him, helpless and discontented. As a result, they may react aggressively, or they may become impervious or anxious. The gentle person, on his part, may develop a false self as a result, along with chronic experiences of weakness and fragility, of non-belonging and loneliness, of being a source of frustration, unwanted, displeasing, misunderstood, and having no place in the world. Deeper strata of suffering and the associated modes of organization touch upon primitive, raw processes which are stamped onto a person's psycho-physical system. Here we will find materials related to regulation and holding, digestion and containment, rhythm and tone; to the tracks along which move the forces of life and death, both in the mind-body and in the interpersonal realm; to a graph staked out by degrees of attention and alertness, a dialectic between engagement and disconnection, between existence and disappearance. These materials cannot be kept apart from the more exposed strata, while the "deep" materials, in their turn, keep showing through the surface – in the shape of idiosyncratic facial expressions or gestures, self-holding through posture and muscle tone, the course of breathing, patterns of attachment, and modes of inter-relating. This is how it is when we look into the mind: all produces all, reveals all, leads into all – surface and depth, past and present, intraper-sonal and interpersonal, mental and physical.

If the parent herself is gentle, the gap diminishes; if her gentleness had the opportunity to be processed, then her gentle children's point of departure will be a better one. Still, they will have to cope with the rest of the world and social surroundings, be in dialogue with their demands and ways of conduct, and experience the collision with coarseness wherever it occurs. It is on the basis of this perspective, rather than in its place, that I will approach the issue from a number of additional angles; to add layer upon layer so as to touch another dimension of the experience of gentle-ness, which thus may come to carry a somewhat different meaning.

Sensitivity and gentleness

What is gentleness? And why do I prefer "gentleness" over "sensitiv-ity"? Below are some thoughts, by no means exhaustive, about gentle-ness, sensitivity, and their interrelations.

In considering the encounter between inside and outside, Freud thought about the need to keep them apart. He described a layer situ-ated between the world and the psyche which comes to protect the liv-ing from an environment that assaults it with stimuli. It works like a shock absorber: soaking up and damping down the stimuli, it only allows them to enter the system in a diminished state, filtered and weakened. To accomplish its goal, this buffer tissue has to sacrifice itself: it becomes inorganic, dead (Freud, 1920). Freud assumed that we are unable to per-ceive reality in its entirety, as it is, undiluted. Too much reality – in his perspective – kills.

Sensitive people, it seems at times, have to cope with an overload of reality.[1] It may be that their buffer, their protective layer, is more delicate or less filtering, or perhaps it simply isn't entirely dead. (Perhaps, if such a layer exists at all, it is never entirely dead in any one of us; rather, it has varying degrees of vitality.) If more stimuli enter them and get absorbed in their bodies and minds, then they may well experience, along with increased injury and pain, a greater vitality and pleasure. How much vitality can one bear? How much pain, how much pleasure? The answers to these questions are different for each and every one of us and depend on the elaborate texture produced by external and internal features: each person's inborn traits, the conditions of the material environment, the broader family and social context, parental holding, maternal and paternal containers, the evolving psyche's own ability to experience goodness and assimilate it, its tendency to internalize the digestive and transformative mechanisms and subsequently to develop the ability to tolerate ambiguity and frustration while suspending the discharge of pain. Though all these are formulated in terms of early life, their influence, manifestation, and change continue throughout a lifetime, and I will return to them at length. For the moment, let's assume that sensitivity confronts the mind with "more", and that the question of which courses this "more" will take depends on the dialectic between these factors, which are mutually formative. It is this dialectic that determines when "more" is overwhelming and when it is regulated; when it is diverted and distorted and when it is repressed and suffocated; when it floods so badly that the system will have to blunt itself or die; when it is permitted to be and, supported by the right tools, become a resource, pure gold, the very ground for connecting with the world.

The world touches us and we feel. All that lives feels, aware or unaware as they may be. More sensitivity – more life: whether good or bad, that will be decided elsewhere. And so, sensitivity is life, or an expression of life. It is the opening up to life, or the closing down, hardening towards it. As such, it covers the whole of the spectrum, from the most subtle to the crude (Eigen, 2004). As it is part of gentleness, I will naturally refer often to sensitivity. It is unquestionably part of the picture, but it doesn't make up the whole of it. For gentleness, I would like to suggest a slightly different position. I propose to see it, in its mature form, as a developmental achievement or value. And this, while considering the complexities associated with the experience of gentleness once it encounters an incompatible external reality, is the perspective I hope to develop.

Sensitivity can manifest itself inclusively, as a basic characteristic, but also as a limited, local phenomenon; a person who has certain sensitivities is not necessarily gentle. Take for example the character Jean-Baptiste Grenouille, eighteenth-century murderer and protagonist of Patrick Suskind's 1985 novel *Perfume* (Suskind, 1985). Grenouille was extraordinarily sensitive to smell, a sensitivity that evolved into a consummate form of art. He was alive to the universe of smell and sensed it at an unsurpassed resolution. He always preferred exhaling to inhaling. The world entered him through his nostrils with a detailed, dense intensity. For eighteen years, incessantly and unconsciously, he suffered the assault of the smells around him, until one day he left the city and realized how unbearable human society and its smells had been to him. The further away he got, the cleaner the air became – and a growing sense of alleviation drew him further away. Eventually he found himself a hidden alcove, remote from anything human. Once he ascertained, through his sense of smell, that neither man nor woman had ever set foot in this space, he decided to stay. He lived in this den for seven years, as if in a grave, curled up in the dark and silence, creeping out every so often to find some meager sustenance. He himself, as he later revealed, carried no smell; lacking an olfactory wrapping (Anzieu, 2016) of his own, he yearned for one and sought for the sources from which to produce it.

Without an olfactory wrapping, he was more exposed to the ambient smells – and they came at him like an attack. In his lair he found respite, as it provided a clear, cool, and quiet sensory envelope. It mainly worked to insulate him, like a capsule leaving the world outside and separate from his inner world. In this capsule, for the first time in his life, he felt truly safe.

Extremely sensitive to the sensory input reaching him from outside and desperate for an envelope, Grenouille, nevertheless, was far from being gentle. From birth his body had endured taxing experiences; it had survived harsh labor and terrible disease with leechlike tenacity. His soul was a moral wasteland, without a grain of compassion or shame. The olfactory wrappings he managed to obtain he exploited for warped, perverse needs: the isolated cave that served as his hideaway, an escape from the burden of human smells, became a cocoon in which he could endlessly indulge his primitive addiction to sensual desire. Though his search for a smell of his own originated in a horrible dread of non-existence, which flared up as soon as he realized he couldn't smell himself (and the first envelope he produced was of a kind that allowed him to pour himself into existence), it soon turned into a quest for the potions that would enable him to blind people in order to subjugate them. And so Grenouille's sensitivity was a limited one which coexisted with forms of imperviousness and coarseness.

While this of course is an extreme illustration, it is not difficult to see that sensitivity and gentleness are not one and the same thing. Gentleness includes sensitivity but is not sensitivity alone. Sensitivity and murderousness can live under the same roof. Gentleness responds to violence with recoil.

Gentleness, injury, and the drive towards the good

Winnicott (1975) described early development as a natural movement between interruption and continuity, between impingement and spontaneous recovery. The infantile entity aims for a round, smooth sense of continuity, one that needs not be conscious of itself. Mental and physical distress threaten to disrupt it, and so they must be taken care of by the mother (or the parent) to prevent it from acting too devastatingly. The good-enough mother invests herself in her baby and adjusts herself to him: almost totally, in the beginning, and later on in a more open-ended manner. She holds both his body and his mind, allowing him to recover from the inevitable injuries of existence. The gradual decline in this adjustment itself is part of the process of attunement and adjustment, in so far as it goes hand in hand with the child's increasing ability to tolerate the world. If all conditions, internal and external alike, enable this process to successfully unfold, then impingements will not end up with fractures and interruptions will not distort the personality. It will, then, grow in peace: alive, creative, not false and not detached from itself.

And still, no matter how devoted and adapted the parental figures, and however good the other conditions, the infant is hurt. Life naturally involves suffering, and the infant gets hurt and recovers, is interrupted and goes on. Eigen (2004) associated this rhythm with sensitivity. He wrote: "Sensitivity is ripped apart by life. There are wounds that never heal – perhaps shouldn't heal. But even these wounds can feed a drive for the better: to create a better world, to be a better person" (p. 19). The basis for ethics, from Eigen's perspective, is responsiveness to sensitivity, or the maturation of sensitive responsiveness (p. 180). I would like to propose gentleness, in its mature state, as a quality that reflects the position of the one who uses her sensitivity in a non-destructive manner, to experience her own and others' sensitivity and to respond to it.

Like many other gentle people, Ron felt fragile and unheld for long years. Experiences related to life's impingements go on rumbling far below the surface of being, even if they are managed relatively well by a strong personality. In Ron's case, they were wounds that had been temporarily overlaid by an as-if-recovery, a short-lived recovery, a recovery enabling normative conduct until it encounters a reality that peels it away. True recovery – the kind that does not function as a patch (Fleischman, 1999) – came later, and it changed his life; but all the cells of his body and mind still remember the hurt. They remain sensitive to it and to its presence – within himself and in others who have suffered similar pain.

A mental layer, once it has been hurt and healed, is unlike one that has never been hurt at all. Some traces will be left on it, and it will be more tremulous, more sensitive in its encounter with the world. Tiny pulses of pain will still make themselves felt through it from time to time. It remembers the wound, and this memory makes it sensitive to its particular pain and to pain as such. In the right context, this makes the mind sensitive to the truth of pain, to the pain of the world.

The injuries of the gentle person are many and frequent, and they engrave themselves in her with great detail. Imperviousness is not a viable possibility for her unless she uses external means that instill it for a while. The widely branched impacts of life push their way into view, whether she likes it or not, very often leaving her with no choice but to become aware. Even when one has not yet found a good way to process suffering and grow from it, even when one doesn't understand the process whereby suffering arises and how this process may be reversed, it is extremely difficult to avoid awareness of the very existence of suffering. And on the condition that one's mind is not too shaky, and provided that external circumstances are reasonably fair, chances are one will seek release. In some cases, she will not settle for superficial healing and will go on to examine herself, reality, and the truth. Gentleness places those endowed with it in a special position: it is not an easy one, but has great virtues.

This book explores gentleness as a way of being and mode of existence. It looks into the effects of the way the gentle person meets his human and non-human surroundings, in light of his specific characteristics. It is aimed at gentle people and at those who live with them: parents, partners, friends, educators, and therapists who wish to understand gentleness and hold it in a slightly different manner. Moving between experience and reflection, I examine the role of the environment in shaping the experience of gentleness and the perceptual-sensory-conscious discrepancy which often exists between the gentle person and his surroundings. I ask what happens when he has to face the sometimes coarse morality of our society, and I consider the path which the Buddha's teaching – as it appears in his discourses and is applied through Vipassana meditation – paves for those who wish to go from the coarse to the subtle. Next, I look into when and how the substances of our sensitivity – the painful and the pleasant – are bound to stand in the way of the growth of personality and spiritual development and when, by contrast, they are vitally necessary and supportive. Thoughts about anxiety, discomfort, and non-belonging – all of which tend to accompany gentle people – take me to one of their life's missions; namely, to rid their gentleness of the fragility, the destructiveness, and the confusion that often get entangled with it and to their struggle to be understood and find themselves a home in this world. Finally I ask: If the environment is so important and the gap so painful, what may we do for the gentle among us – ourselves and others – to create a better, more adjusted environment? Here I define attention and state of mind as environment and examine the possibility of turning them into a sensitively adapted, attuned inner space in which gentleness is delicately held instead of being crushed and repressed.

The personal stories I have chosen to include offer glances into the living, quivering core of gentleness. They illustrate something of its challenge and its beauty and suggest how life's impingements may transform into awareness and compassion, and pain into a noble pain. By means of all this, I hope to awaken the tenderness and lucidity that gentleness invokes. My hope is that future encounters with gentleness, however camouflaged by the realities of one's coping with it, will engender love.

Note

1 Here, I use the word *reality* as referring to the universe of stimuli – not necessarily as a synonym of *truth*. However, this is not the case in all contexts in which I use it.

References

Anzieu, D. (2016). *The Skin-Ego*. London: Karnac.

Barnea-Astrog, M. (2015). Internal holding, external holding: three experiences in primitive fear of annihilation. *Hebrew Psychology*. Accessed May 18, 2015 at: www.hebpsy.net/articles.asp?id=3252

Bick, E. (1968). The experience of the skin in early object-relations. *International Journal of Psycho-Analysis*, *49*: 484–486.

Eigen, M. (2004). *The Sensitive Self*. Middletown, CT: Wesleyan University.

Epstein, M. (2013). *The Trauma of Everyday Life*. New York: Penguin.

Fleischman, P. R. (1999). Healing the healer. In: *Karma and Chaos* (pp. 40–53). Onalska, WA: Vipassana Research Publication.

Freud, S. (1920). Beyond the pleasure principle. *S.E.*, *18:* 1–64.

Klein, M. (1946). Notes on some schizoid mechanisms. *International Journal of Psychoanalysis*, *27*: 99–110.

Kolker, S. (2009). Introduction to "Fear of breakdown". In: D. W. Winnicott, *True Self, False Self: Essays, 1935–1963*, edited by E. Berman (pp. 287–291). Tel Aviv: Am Oved.

Ogden, T. H. (2004). *The Primitive Edge of Experience*. Lanham, MD: Rowman & Littlefield.

Suskind, P. (1985). *Perfume: The Story of a Murderer*. New York: Knopf.

Symington, J. (1985). The survival function of primitive omnipotence. *International Journal of Psycho-Analysis, 66*: 481–487.

Winnicott, D. W. (1974). Fear of breakdown. *International Review of Psycho-Analysis, 1*: 103–107.

Winnicott, D. W. (1975). Primary maternal preoccupation. In: *Through Paediatrics to Psycho-Analysis* (pp. 300–305). London: Hogarth & the Institute of Psycho-Analysis.

Chapter 2

The path of gentleness

I began practicing Vipassana about eighteen or nineteen years ago, when I was in my mid-twenties. For the first time, I met with a perspective that acknowledged suffering as a feature of existence, that recognized the great seriousness required for any work with the psyche, its complexes and winding ways. For the first time, here was an approach that did not tell me to toughen up, to get more sturdy, but said: Your sensitivity is welcome. Your gentleness is a virtue, and it does not have to come inevitably with a verdict of misery and separateness. Here was a way of seeing things that says it isn't possible to be in touch with deep truth without developing sensitivity; one that expressly aims to increase awareness of the nuances of experience and to sharpen the resolution through which reality is perceived, while at the same time offering the gentle person (any person, in fact) the necessary counterbalance – namely, the resources she needs to cope with her sensitivity and what arises from one moment to the next once it comes into contact with the world.

I met people who followed the path of gentleness, modest, quiet people who were not looking for a stage or to make a name for themselves. They were unpretentious and obviously not ideal, but certainly happier and wiser than me: each with their own personality, each at their own specific and constantly changing point in the process. Though my first years of practice were difficult and turbulent, something inside me recognized these people and began to feel that there was somewhere to go. That the investigation of the psyche did not have to be riddled with torture and loneliness; that it is supposed to teach about the sources of suffering and loneliness even as it undoes them. I began to feel that not only was there someone who understood what I was seeing – or trying to see – but that there were those who saw a great deal more than I, and all they wanted was to give me, into these very hands which were still getting messed up with a lot of nonsense, a tool which would allow me to study myself and thereby gradually work my way out of this mess.

This tool, Vipassana, cultivates gentleness. It does so by following the Buddha's path: by means of practicing a realistic way of seeing things, ethical behavior, and meditation.[1] I would like to say some things about this path and how perspective, behavior, and mental cultivation feature in it. I'll show how this nurtures gentleness in a manner that enables it to shed its often concomitant fragility and destructiveness and how, once divested of these, gentleness turns into a virtue and a value. Referring to Buddhist ethics, and in the light of some of the messages our secular modern or postmodern society infuses into the gentle layers of the mind, I would like to discuss the social-cultural context as one factor that may either clash with or support gentleness.

Behavior, meditation, and wisdom

Buddhist ethics aims at a mode of being that is in harmony with the world. This implies that an action is considered right[2] if it is beneficial and does no harm, if it contributes to clear vision and liberation and not to blindness and suffering. The behavioral aspect of this relates to a person's external activities: his physical actions, his way of speaking, and his way of life. For these to be called "right", they should agree with a simple, logical, and universal morality. This involves avoiding killing or physically hurting living creatures, avoiding appropriating something without permission, avoiding inappropriate sexual conduct, avoiding intoxicating substances, and avoiding harmful speech: speech that is false or misleading, slanderous and divisive, harsh, assaulting or aggressive, sarcastic or gossipy, or frivolous speech which is wasteful of one's own and others' time. It is therefore good to earn one's livelihood in ways that neither involve any of the above behaviors nor encourage others to engage in them. Buddhist morality, however, is not merely a negative, avoidant one. Once we take out the harmful behaviors, we are left with the positive, virtuous ones, and these we strive to cultivate.

It's obvious that when someone pushes the person ahead of them in the line at the supermarket checkout, she is acting crudely compared to another person who is patiently waiting for her turn. A person who asks his neighbor if she doesn't mind him picking some lemons from the tree in her backyard acts more gently than another who simply decides to fill two baskets with mandarins from the orchard abutting the road. A person who makes some sexist remark to a woman passing him in the street acts coarsely in comparison with a person who looks at the same woman in a friendly way and with respect, or who at least refrains from expressing his lust out loud. A thoughtful and sensitive manner of talking that tries not to harm oneself or another is more gentle than speaking harshly and aggressively. It's also clear that it is more likely for a person to behave crudely, in one or more of these ways, when they are drunk than when sober, and that dealing in arms or drugs is a cruder form of earning a living than being a carpenter, teaching math, or nursing. So far so good: teachings aimed at moral conduct are certainly off to a good start. But if this was all that the Buddha's teachings were about, they wouldn't have amounted to the teachings of a Buddha. Physical and verbal behavior reflect the mind's activity, and the fruits of this behavior – for the one performing it – are the direct outcome of the mental activity that underlines it.

> Mind precedes all phenomena, mind matters most, mind is the source.
> If you speak or act with an impure mind,
> Suffering will follow you
> As the wheel of a bullock cart follows behind the bullock.
>
> Mind precedes all phenomena, mind matters most, mind is the source.
> If you speak or act with a pure mind,
> Happiness will follow you
> As a shadow that never departs.
>
> (Dhp 1–2, translated from the Pāli by William
> Hart. In: Barnea-Astrog, 2017, p. 61)

The statement that mind precedes all phenomena carries a number of meanings, but the main one is that mental action is action in the full sense of that word and has actual effects in the world (Barnea-Astrog, 2017). If we delve further into the implications of this idea, we will find that it is not merely suffering and happiness that are a product of the mind, but – as the text explains – all phenomena. Through an infinity of connections between an infinity of factors, which we are unable to follow, stretching to the present from a past both recent and remote, the circumstances of our lives arise from our mental actions. Our bodies, personalities, abilities, and limitations, the qualities of the human and material environment into which we are poured and from which we constantly feed – they all are born in this way. This isn't an omnipotent-magical notion – "if I just think of a million dollars, I'll have it" – but an insight concerning the natural relations between cause and effect. It is based on the understanding that mind and matter are interdependent, produce each other, and flow from each other in complicated ways that nonetheless have a lucid regularity: everything that is rooted in blindness, desire, and hate results in suffering and bondage. Everything that is rooted in non-blindness, non-desire, and non-hate leads to happiness and liberation. This logic implies that although someone contemplating a million dollars out of greed may actually succeed in making a million dollars in some concrete way, her greed, as such, will have less desirable results.

It is difficult to trace back to what specifically brought us to a certain psycho-physical moment, but we will find something important even when considering things that are quite accessible to the eye. A mind full of lust will produce a lustful gaze. A mind filled with hate will move hate around and throughout its surroundings. A mind full of envy, greed, contempt, bitterness, fear, guilt, depression, laziness, restlessness, or doubt produces compatible behaviors, whether more dramatic or less distinct (Barnea-Astrog, 2017). This then brings us to the meditative part of the path: If we don't train our mind and increase its ability to control itself, on the one hand, and if we don't work with it, on the other hand, to begin to undo blindness, hate, and desire, to dissolve envy, greed, contempt, bitterness, fear, guilt, depression, laziness, restlessness, and doubt, we cannot expect ourselves to behave in a truly moral way.

First we need a modicum of self-restraint, which will enable us to start avoiding physical and verbal expressions of the harmful impulses that arise in us. The ability to gain control depends on concentration and calmness. At a more subtle level, the ability to focus and control the mind will also help suspend and repress destructive mental actions; control alone, however, is not enough. Anyone who has ever tried to work with and investigate the mind knows how hard it is to get the mind to let go of bad habits that have become ingrained. Even where we manage to overcome their behavioral expressions for a stretch of time, their roots run deep and they are always waiting, threatening to rise up and resume control. (One only has to think of those who managed to quit smoking, and fifteen years later, picked it up again.)

The depths of the mind are swarming with destructive elements, and they pull our strings unconsciously, from behind the scenes. Our minds are ruled by insipidness, confusion, illusion, and neglect. Residues of earlier, harmful actions, they exist in us like a default option. They fuel themselves, taking root outside our field of vision, pushing us to act crudely and violently, more or less bluntly, towards ourselves and others. Everything that is habitual in nature has the tendency to root and multiply. The study of the mind has shown us this. Neuropsychological research has shown us. Nature has. In order to set ourselves free from violence, we must free ourselves from the harmful habits that generate it. We must invest ourselves in a practice that enables the mind to recognize what harms it, to become strong enough to avoid following it, and to gradually begin to dissolve it.

This requires scrupulous analysis. In this sense, the focusing and calming of the mind are like the sharpening of the surgeon's scalpel, and if we want to reach into the depths of the mind, they are fundamentally vital. The sharpened knife – to various degrees – is attention or awareness, directed systematically and thoroughly at the internal reality and its constantly ongoing processes: processes of consciousness-perception-sensation-reaction, processes of mind and matter, interconnected though complex relations. An awareness that is equal to this kind of labor must be equipped with an understanding of the processes it examines. It must observe their constant changing, the fact that they are neither personal nor essential, that they are all interdependent, conditioned and conditioning – and as such, fated to perish and bound up with dissatisfaction and suffering. In Buddhist teachings, this is a realistic view. When we direct our attention to our inner reality but do so from an unrealistic, confused, illusive, or simply dull perspective, it will not be much use. Where our perspective is dull, we will not see deeply. We will not identify the nature of the processes and phenomena. If our perspective is confused, rather than undoing the tangle, we may well tighten and further complicate it. When I am angry at someone and try to look at my anger by revisiting the annoying event again and again, in detail, picturing the people who supposedly made me angry and accusing them, all I am doing is fanning my anger and its causes without really understanding it, let alone dissolving it.

All parts of the path necessarily interweave and are mutually dependent. Right behavior[3] is key to right concentration,[4] and right concentration is fundamental to the development of wisdom.[5] But these parts of the triangle interrelate reciprocally and in various directions. The ability to calm and focus the mind gains from our striving to act morally and at the very same time forms the basis of such conduct and deepens it. A calm, focused, and disciplined mind supports self-control and thereby helps us avoid harmful behaviors, but it also produces the conditions to develop the ability to be aware. Awareness is ready and willing to examine things in depth when supported by a realistic view and understanding. Proper understanding of phenomena and processes naturally leads to ethical behavior and mental equanimity.[6] Equanimity stabilizes and sharpens the mind and allows it to see more.

Any other structure, in the present context, will eventually collapse or prove insufficient. So, for instance, immoral behavior is the result of a craving, restless mind, and a craving, restless mind cannot be stable, sharp, or clear. Although it is quite possible to focus and calm the mind in the absence of a moral basis, according to the Buddha, these are superficial focus and calm which do not contribute to real progress on the path leading to a total removal of the mind's negative accumulations. Similarly, one may train the mind to look inward systematically without equipping it with sufficient knowledge – however primary and minimal – concerning the origins of suffering and becoming and without instructing it on how to wisely face what it finds inside, but one should not expect that the fruits of such introspection will be anything like those of introspection supported by what the Buddha called "right view". When all parts of the path grow together, then gentleness of action nurtures gentleness of mind, and gentleness of mind nurtures gentleness of action. Stability nurtures gentleness; gentleness nurtures clarity; clarity nurtures stability and gentleness. Together, they enable the mind to lay bare its deepest habits and to shake them up from the core. "Ethics can be superimposed from the outside only up to a point", writes Eigen (2004, p. 180). "Its deeper grounding is in maturation of sensitive responsiveness". From the outside in and from the inside out, from the behavioral to the mental and from the mental to the behavioral: If we don't want to cut corners in ethics, both of these movements must take place at one and the same time.

The necessary equipment

Let us now direct our attention to those parts of the path that touch upon awareness and wisdom.

Eigen wrote: "We can't take too much reality. Our equipment simply is not up to it. If we are lucky, persistent, patient, hungry enough for the real, our equipment grows into the job, building more capacity to work with what is" (2004, p. 8). From the vantage point of Vipassana, the equipment needed for coping with reality is related to a combination of awareness of the object of sensitivity (the felt, the experienced) and a certain attitude towards it that one must cultivate. It is the mind's default function to act on the pleasure principle: to be attracted by the pleasant and to try and keep away from the unpleasant. When this is how it acts, the mind is in distress, unstable, hanging from a thread. The world touches it and it is shaken, yearns and clings, constantly reacting out of ignorance, with desire and hate; and in each such reactive moment, it ties itself further into the tangle of its vulnerability in the face of a precarious reality. In the Buddha's teachings, it is due to this state of affairs that we suffer; but this is not ordained by fate, and we are not unable to change it. The mind can train itself to experience without pulling or pushing away: to sharpen itself and be attentive to the subtleties of the components of experience, to observe how they arise and pass away; to recognize their temporary and inessential nature, understand how they are linked with suffering, and stop identifying with them. As it becomes more proficient at doing this, it gets better at sensing and opening to the flow of stimuli that touch or invade it – and yet it gradually stops being hurt by these encounters: it stays firm in the face of a reality it experiences in a less distorted, more direct way.

Our harmful habits are related to imperviousness, or to the way in which our sensitivity meets reality and reacts to it. Imperviousness conceals; sensitivity meets reality through the marks of its injuries. When it seems that a certain woman's level of sensitivity is on the relatively impervious side of the scale, this means that her encounter with the world occurs through dullness. Imperviousness and dullness do not result in an absence of reaction; they dictate certain habits of reaction. Imperviousness and dullness do not rid one of greed and hatred – they form a cover below which greed and hatred teem. Hence, one of the first tasks in such a case will involve sharpening the resolution of sensation and perception. (Dullness sometimes protects against trauma. In such cases, resolution must be sharpened in a cautious manner, and with proper assistance.) When, by contrast, sensitivity is high, it is often experienced as exaggerated, as an attack. If it is not accompanied by the appropriate complementary equipment, it becomes painful. Here, the most urgent task is related to the ability to live in peace with the experience of "more". One way or another, no matter what the point of departure is, this, in the end, is the objective: to reduce the discrepancy between reality's impact and our ability to process that impact; to develop the mental equipment to be able to manage with what is, and eventually – "if we are lucky, persistent, patient, hungry enough for the real" (Eigen, 2004, p. 8) – to attain full awareness and perfect mental equilibrium.

Gentleness and destructiveness

Gentleness includes sensitivity, and when the equipment to keep it in balance is insufficiently developed, an experience of vulnerability or fragility emerges. This experience is linked to the fear of one who has already been hurt by life from being hurt once more.

While the combination of fragility and gentleness appears quite natural to us, the less obvious pair of gentleness and destructiveness is also quite common. Gentleness fundamentally abhors violence, but, like any other mind, the mind of a gentle person in whom some essential inner struggles have yet to be settled, whose depths still churn, overflowing with undigested shreds of experience, full of obscure corners and unmapped territory – such a mind carries a considerable amount of destructiveness. The more obvious manifestations of destructiveness we all know: people lead lives that involve clear and evident harm, engage in negative relationships, develop bad eating and sleeping habits, knowingly ingest all kinds of substances that damage them physically or mentally, or they embezzle and cheat and pay a heavy price. To the less visible formations of destructiveness we can attribute all undermining elements that attack the psyche and its links to reality from within: envy and greed, self-castigation and judgmentalness, deadening rationalism, self-abasement and doubt of the deluding kind; helplessness, neglect and laziness, despair, hate, and vengefulness. A person can be both very delicate and full of passion and turmoil, desperately in need of a sensitive and gentle environment whose nuances harmonize with her own, but also impulsive and wild and in constant search of intense arousal. The mind is far from being uniform: sparkling vitality and forces of destruction weave together in it, either feeding it and making it grow or gripping and suffocating it. How do these forces interrelate? The dynamics of the instincts I am not competent to deal with in any comprehensive way; still, in this limited context and in the light of the appearance of these forces concurrently with gentleness, I would like to propose some thoughts.

Freud (1920) drew a distinction between the death instincts and the life instincts but also reached a confusing conclusion: the forces that aim to preserve life are nothing but the slaves of death. It is true that these forces, by following the reality principle, help one to conduct herself in a manner that safeguards her from the dangers associated with the clash between her desires and the circumstances. But all they are after is for one to march towards her death in her own particular way, fending off every danger that crosses her path: struggling, that is, against the chances she might die in any other way than the one that is inherently her own. The sexual instincts, by contrast, Freud defines as life instincts and the only ones that do not pull towards conservation and death. Paradoxically, however, if they were allowed unhindered expression, they would surely endanger the individual every so often. When we add insights from the Buddha's teachings to these Freudian ones, the picture of reality changes a little. From a Buddhist point of view, desire as well as destructiveness come under the factor of *taṇhā*: craving or thirst. The writings distinguish three types of thirst: the thirst for sensual pleasures or for attractive sensual objects; the thirst for becoming as such, for life, for certain states of existence or self-identity; and the thirst for non-becoming, the wish to cease being or the wish to escape hated objects and situations and to be free of them. Some compare the life instincts to the thirst for becoming and the death instincts to the thirst for non-becoming (Payutto, 1995). But in the Buddha's teachings, these factors are not essentially that much opposed. Sure, each of them points towards a different domain of meaning and relates to different mental actions, leading to different outcomes, but ultimately thirst is thirst: it is a force that produces life and kills simultaneously, a force that fuels the chain of becoming, in which decay, death, and suffering, too, are links (Barnea-Astrog, 2017). The sexual instincts are clearly connected to the thirst of sensual desire, but they are equally bound up with the thirst for becoming and creating life. The instincts of self-preservation are linked to having one's grip on life, but since they also seek, as Freud pointed out, to take the organism back to an inorganic state, they are also associated with the thirst for non-becoming. And while desire, passion, impulsivity, and the need for arousal are expressions of the life instincts, they may equally be the basis of violent actions against body and mind. Violence is naturally tied to the death instincts: but an instinct is an instinct and desire is inherent to it – and isn't desire an expression of the instincts of life? And so we cannot uncouple the two groups of instincts. These are directed towards creation and those towards annihilation; these tend towards development and those towards destruction – yet all are subject to the pleasure principle and the repetition compulsion. In Buddhist terms, all are at play in the field of becoming and decay, fueling the Samsaric cycle in which suffering is the outcome of ignorance and thirst.

Destructiveness, therefore, can be a product of formations of desire or formations of hatred. It may be experienced as something that sets us on fire or, on the contrary, extinguishes; it may take a persecutory-splitting shape but also a depressive-depleting one. Either way, in the case of a gentle person, one thing destructiveness expresses is her struggle to survive in a rough world. It may reflect her reaction to primary figures from her early life who found it hard to perceive her gentleness and hold it softly – internalized figures who now batter her gentleness from within. It may come to express her efforts to live in a world in which such figures exist, a world whose imperatives, as Eigen put it, rip sensitivity apart.

Nina: an unconscious struggle between the gentleness of mind and internalized social norms

On the psyche's stage the instincts of life and death wrestle: Sensual desire, the desire to exist, and the desire to not-exist push hard, striving to set fire, to fuel the flames, to extinguish and drain things of meaning. All are in dialogue with sensitivity. All, to some extent or another, put pressure on gentleness. It is against the background of these pushy, domineering intra-psychic forces, that the cultural-social context into which a person is born and raised is important. Social values and conventions leave their mark on the accepted style of parenting, on parents' perception of reality and their mental fabric. These in turn produce the individual's closest surroundings at the beginning of life: the setting that influences the development of his mental equipment, which dictates his style of dealing with reality. In time, as the child grows up and comes into contact with ever-widening circles of the external world, these values and conventions, the decrees of society, affect him more directly.

Eigen (2014) wrote about psychoanalytic sensitivity in a psychopathic world and about the price paid by those who struggle to study their sensitivity in a world that does not sufficiently value it. The sensitivity he described is a sensitivity directed outward – towards others – and inward – towards oneself, a sensitivity that feels the substances of being. He referred to the development of caring as the moral base necessary for living together, to the need for "sensitivity to the sensitive core of living beings" (p. 174). This is an ethics of sensitivity that involves responsiveness to sensitivity – something that seems so out of tune with a world in which the goal of both individual and group is "to be number one" (p. 178).

Being number one is not the only objective hallowed by our culture. The individual who grows up in it absorbs a variety of messages, not a few of which contradict and trample gentleness. To illustrate these messages and the way they clash with gentleness, I will introduce Nina and how she developed in the face of the prevailing attitude to sexuality. Her story shows how such a clash can affect the mind. I will narrate it while referring to an alternative ethics, that of the Buddha's path.

***

I first met Nina when she was about thirty, studying for her master's degree. We met once a week for a period of two years, and some years later, we briefly resumed our meetings in order to work through a certain situation that she was coping with. Nina had started practicing Vipassana even before beginning our therapy, in her late twenties. Initially she practiced Vipassana in a more limited way, not yet committing herself to its universal morality (*sīla*), which, as mentioned, includes abstention from what is defined as "sexual misconduct". Sincerely seeking the right partner, she moved from one relationship into another. Sometimes these were serious and meaningful; at other times they were entered in a rush and fleeting. Outwardly, everything seemed ordinary: Nina behaved according to the notions and norms of her surroundings. But, in time, as her awareness of her bodily sensations and their mental concomitants grew stronger and subtler (like me, she practiced the form of Vipassana as taught by S. N. Goenka, which places special emphasis on body sensations), she began noticing that something inside her disconnected at the most intimate moments. Gradually, attention to her physical-mental experience of disconnection exposed her to profound underlying feelings of being hurt. She was shocked by this direct realization of how disconnection was serving to protect her against these feelings, and she became wide awake to the fact that she put herself in painful situations, repeatedly and on her own, however unconscious initiative.

Nina grew up with parents who acted in sexually explicit ways with each other in front of their children. These behaviors were within the norms of modern western secular life, although on the high end of the scale. They were perceived and presented as proof of the parents' love, their healthy relationship and sexual passion, which is a good and natural thing when directed at a loving partner. The message was that this was how it ought to be: that it was healthy and right – even necessary – to be sexual. From the onset of adolescence, Nina felt conflicted. She was looking for a partner with whom she could be sexual, the way she learned at home; yet, at the same time, terrible anxiety would take over whenever a man who she didn't consider a candidate for a relationship would direct sexual attention at her. Every look with even a touch of lust she experienced as invasive, exacting, evil, making her feel disgusted and afraid. She was worried about looking sexual, but she also wanted to and felt she ought to. This conflict raged inside her, deep and unsettled. She gave herself to too many sexual partners. She dressed rather provocatively – almost without noticing. She was beset by a fear of sexual assault, and her body and mind reacted disproportionately to everyday events which other people would not interpret as sexually threatening.

Among other issues we examined in the time we spent together were her senses of disconnection and injury, her yearning and conflict, and her fear of further injury. In the countertransference, as concerns this context, I noticed how I tended to see her shifting, alternating from girl to woman and back again, and from a sexual creature to an asexual one. She usually came to our meetings dressed in wide and shabby clothes, a training suit and slippers (ostensibly relaxed, the sort of thing you wear at home; with hindsight: maybe also in order to seem asexual facing the "parent"). But when she came in on her way to or from some other activity, I saw how she presented herself to the rest of the world. My changing perception of her was not necessarily a function of her dress – sometimes it even clashed with her appearance. It was, however, exactly due to these oscillations in her looks that I came to see her external appearance as yet another expression of what was happening deep inside her.

In the meantime, Nina went on practicing Vipassana and grew older. Slowly she became aware of some other things. She became aware of what she felt when she was near her parents when they acted in their customary sexual manner, and she realized how this had been not simply embarrassing or uncomfortable for her but actually harmful. She began to understand her own behavior: on the one hand, her parents' sexually explicit demeanor pushed her to try and re-create this form of sexuality – having been presented as a value in its own right, an objective or a convention that must be followed – and on the other hand, it made her anxious of the invasion of similar mental substances (which she experienced as toxic) from her surroundings. Consequently she evolved a rigid set of boundaries and divisions meant to define who was to be allowed to see her as a sexual creature and who was not. This, apparently, was the way in which she dealt with the blurred boundaries that were the result of her parents' sexual conduct – which, though not directed at her, took place in her presence. At the same time she reproduced this very same situation, again and again, of being invaded by a lust that was not truly aimed at her and only happened in her presence; this she contrived by unconsciously stirring herself into intimate situations while partly disconnecting from herself.

Nina did not use her meditation practice to reach an autobiographical explanation for the way in which her life was playing itself out, nor did she try to identify the ostensibly responsible situations or people. During the first, main period of her therapy with me, too, no insights about the origins of her repetitively destructive behavior came up. These only emerged years later, maturing and manifesting themselves to her at their own pace. A long time before that, however, when she understood the damage she was doing to herself, she changed her behavior radically, so that deep-seated layers of perceptual distortion and the associated suffering started to dissolve and gradually disappear from her life. Auto-biographical insight, in Nina's case, was of secondary importance. It appeared at a key moment of clarification, to tie up the loose ends, a long time after she had set herself free from the harmful pattern. Sensory-conscious insight, however, was vital.

Nina's case can be considered in various contexts. I would like to dis-cuss it, presently, from the point of view of the pain originating in the encounter between a gentle psyche and a coarse but socially approved reality. Nina's sexual conduct as such didn't qualify as especially wan-ton; it was normative. While her way of dressing may have attracted the attention of men, it would not be a reason for ordinary people to raise an eyebrow. Her parents' behavior was mostly not considered offensive in their own milieu. Such things run smoothly through western secular society without much further ado. But for Nina, the bluntness was too much.

The cultural norms of Nina's parental home blotted out her sensitivi-ties and went against them. Clashing with her gentleness, they caused confusion and difficult struggles – some conscious and some uncon-scious. No one perceived and respected her sensitivities, acknowledged them and cherished them as intelligent and valuable. There was no one and nothing to make the connection with suitable attitudes and norms. In these circumstances, even she herself could not make attentive contact with what she sensed. She was able to abandon the pattern in which she was stuck only after some years of daily meditation and a therapeu-tic process. Two things happened in parallel: She became aware of her physical sensations and the associated mental contents – her sense of disconnection and her feelings in the presence of her parents' behavior – without rejecting and denying them, without escaping or fanning them or interpreting them prematurely. At the same time she became exposed to a setting whose norms and values were in line with her sensitivities.

Buddhist thinking about right sexual conduct has a broader reach than some of its current definitions in our society, and since mental behavior, not merely physical or verbal behavior, forms the very core of Buddhist ethics, a more refined approach is in order when considering the issue. Behaviorally speaking, in this approach, inappropriate sexual conduct is not only about sexual predatoriness or the betrayal of a spouse but any sexual behavior outside a relationship based on love and long-term commitment.[7] As concerns Nina, even if in the first years of her Vipas-sana practice she did not fully follow this path, it helped her, when the time was ripe, to break – at least at the level of behavior – the vicious cycle by which she was repeatedly recreating the hurtful circumstances.

However, and as said, another extraneous element played a valuable role: this was the very fact of being exposed to a different environment with different values and conventions from the ones with which she had been raised – an environment in which she finally felt protected, where gentleness and sincere (rather than dogmatic or forced) modesty are appreciated; where sexual activity is not taken for granted or treated casually; where teachers are expected to relate to their students as though they were their children – in the present context: not to be sexually involved with them – boundaries are more clear. As Buddhist morality includes uncompromising mental scrutiny, it is not merely behavioral. It is not a repressive moralism, it does not function like lip service, and it isn't superficial. Authority figures who espouse these values are not supposed to cast a lustful gaze at their students. They will not allow such passions to flare up – even if they arise in them – and certainly not express them in action.

This may sound naïve; perhaps a form of idealization or denial. Human nature is what it is, and instincts are instincts. They can never be fully controlled or fundamentally altered. But if this is what we settle for, then we agree with Freud, who believed no mental phenomenon can escape the instincts' domination (Pelled, 2005, p. 51). We accept that "whoever understands the human mind knows that [. . .] we can never give anything up; we only exchange one thing for another" and that "what appears to be a renunciation is really the formation of a substitute or surrogate" (Freud, 1908, p. 145). We agree, in other words, that we are fated to be forever propelled by desire. If this is so, then what can the Buddha's path hold out to us, with its absolute dedication to guiding the mind from its enslavement to the pleasure principle (which originates in ignorance and leads to suffering) towards liberation from clinging to the pleasurable and the painful, to becoming and annihilation? There are, of course, teachers – including those who call themselves "Buddhists" – who develop sexual feelings for and relations with their students – more or less offensively, more or less openly, receiving more or less criticism or legitimation. And yet I believe that in settings like these, where a teacher is supposed to serve his students by conveying the Buddha's words in a way that is as clear of distortions as possible and as minimally affected by personal interests as possible, the ideal must be explicit, well understood, and strictly followed. Personal practice must penetrate deeply enough to allow this, and the school or institution has to give its support (for instance, by means of uncompromising standards in the appointment and further development of teachers and by means of regulations that encourage transparency and clarity). In my personal experience, this is not wishful thinking but something that can be achieved; it was exactly this possibility, and the resulting clarity of boundaries, that Nina experienced. In this environment, she was no longer exposed to the danger that the less conscious layers of her mind identified in other places, and the pressure to behave in a manner that contradicted her vulnerability was removed. In time, the screen that was the result of the clash between inside and outside vanished, and her view became more lucid, allowing her to discern the surrounding dynamics and the way they connected with her own, internal ones.

***

Fragility is related to primitive anxieties and forces of self that cling to life and attempt to conserve it. Destructiveness is related to residues of hate directed at inner and outer reality. Squeezed between them, gentleness can only flourish when they relent. Until such a moment, the struggles that characterize mental life are hard – intolerably so at times.

The eightfold path taught by the Buddha advances from coarse to subtle: from the behavioral to the mental, from blunt to sharp, from the overt to the nearly hidden. A person starts along his way and must cope with the more solid, violent elements. He braves the storms they cause, arising from body and mind and revealing, underneath, less solid and less violent layers. Working with these as well, he discovers ever more subtle realities, the nuances of mental strata, components and processes that were hitherto concealed but no longer are. Here and there again an internal volcano erupts violently – but his mind is already stronger, able to look into the depths at a high resolution.

This is how the path refines. It is also called the "noble path", since those who progress far enough along it become, sooner or later, noble people. A noble person is also a gentle person – but his gentleness is mature and developed. It is simple, clean, and sound, clear of fragility and destructiveness and conflict. The noble person is aware of her experiences and sees them as they are, in their true nature, and therefore doesn't react to them with either hatred or desire. Such a person is sharp, is well attuned, and recoils from violence; at some point she is no longer capable of acting with violence – whether internal or external, of any kind – as the materials that stir violence have been annihilated in her. This process takes time, and everyone who engages in it starts at a different point. We are unable to determine where we begin, and we cannot tell in advance the pace and manner in which we proceed. Not everyone who walks this path is sensitive or gentle, but everyone who walks it advances towards gentleness: gentleness as a virtue, healthy gentleness, appropriate gentleness – neither passive, nor weak, nor shattering.

Beyond mindfulness

Buddhist teachings in their various streams and variations have in recent decades filtered into the western psychological – and pseudo-psychological – discourse. One such manifestation is what these days goes by the name of "mindfulness". When this term is used, one must carefully distinguish between two senses. One refers simply to a state of consciousness or a universal mental quality of awareness, and it is expressed in turning attention to one or more specific elements of experience, with the aim of doing so inquisitively and non-judgmentally. The other sense of mindfulness is a translation of the Pāli word *sati*,[8] and it points at systematic meditation practice. As such, it is synonymous with *sammā-sati*, right mindfulness, the seventh part of the eightfold path. This important part of the Buddha's teachings concerns the establishment of awareness (*satipaṭṭhāna*) of the body and its sensations, the mind and its contents. It is a very specific, unmistakable type of awareness: it involves developing a non-reactive quality vis-à-vis all experience, a non-reaction which leans on a direct understanding of the nature of experience, and is necessarily tied to a thorough investigation of the mind-body and the gradual dissolution of its defilements. This kind of awareness, therefore, cannot come about in detachment from the remaining seven components of the path. These, as said, refer to a universal ethics, the sharpening and calming of the mind, and the development of a realistic and clear point of view.

In the Pāli canon – the writings attributed to the Buddha and some of his preeminent disciples – the general word for meditation is *bhāvanā*, mental development or cultivation.[9] This, in the present context, is tantamount to techniques that offer systematic mental training. Instructions in such a technique, today, will sound something like this: "Pay attention to your breath, from one moment to the next, coming in and coming out . . . Each time your mind is distracted, return to your breathing . . .", or: "Focus all your attention on your belly . . . (or your nose, or any other place) . . . whenever your mind is distracted, return to your belly . . .", and so on. Both within the domain of Buddhism and outside it, there are countless techniques of meditation. Some use mantras, some guided imagination, manipulations of energies, noticing experience while walking or while eating a raisin. Meditation is an enormous category which includes vast amounts of specific cases, all manner of tools to achieve different goals: Sometimes they only differ marginally; at other times they are light years apart. Even if we narrow it down to the family of techniques aimed at improving awareness of the constantly changing flow of experience without exerting any influence, the family we will find is large. It is therefore useful to observe that not every way in which we develop our mind is meditation and that not each invitation to pay attention to what happens inside us is *sati* or *satipaṭṭhāna*. In order to demonstrate this, I will briefly mention a few central psychoanalytic notions concerning the therapist's state of mind and quality of attention.

Freud instructed psychoanalysts to develop their ability for open and non-selective attention. He told his colleagues to try not to let their expectations, inclinations, and hopes (including the hope to heal or bring change) determine to what they paid attention, what they registered, and how they perceived this. Otherwise, he said, they will have missed valuable information and are bound to falsify the details that they do pick up (Freud, 1912). Bion (1988, 1970) took these ideas a long way further. He attempted to achieve self-imposed blindness to past and future, memory and desire (Grotstein, 2000),[10] while also striving to abandon – in addition to old patterns, prejudices, wishes, and expectations – the very need to understand. If we assume that the patient we encounter today is the same one we did yesterday, it is the wrong patient we are meeting, he said. He invited psychoanalysts to develop the ability to dwell in a space without grip, without knowledge, a fragile space marked by a sense of danger, which requires non-religious faith (F). It is only from such a space that the living truth, contact with the unknowable reality (O), can arise and come into being by itself, unmediated by active will.

Bion (1962) described a model of relations between container and contained, one in which a living and dynamic space processes (whether successfully or not) emotional contents. He described a function of mental processing, the alpha function, whose main feature is that it is neither defined nor known. This alpha function includes a factor he termed *reverie* – a state of mind which is open to receive the emotionally charged material another person projects into it. These materials – good or bad, replete with love or with hatred, wished-for or dreaded; mainly dreaded – then linger in a processing-digesting mental locus until they transform, and from being toxic they become useful (to the one who projected them to begin with). An alpha function that works well will process the components of experience in a way that allows for a healthy exchange with reality, one that leads to truth and growth.

Winnicott (1975, 1987) discussed the state of mind required of the mother during the infant's first weeks of life, a state of deep immersion which, anywhere other than in this particular condition, would surely be considered pathological. A mother in this state, ideally speaking, identifies with and is directed towards her child from moment to moment, attentive to its signals, and adapts herself in a natural way that requires no external knowledge. She holds the baby both physically and mentally, and in so doing she provides a healthy place in which the baby can recover from the afflictions that are the inevitable result of the encounter with the world entailed by life. The infant's characteristics and inclinations can express themselves spontaneously and authentically in these conditions and develop without being pushed too hard or twisted.

Taking his cue from Bion, Grotstein, and Sandler in this context, Ogden (2009) refers to talking that is a form of dreaming, to waking-dreaming, to a state of mind that, rather than aiming to bring the unconscious to consciousness, allows the conscious to become unconscious. He describes a space in which conscious experience passes into the domain of the other, richer processes of thinking involved in unconscious psychological work (Ogden, 2009, p. 6). This kind of emotional processing, observation, and experience, in which patient and analyst immerse themselves, generates "particular ways of being with, and communicating with, another person that could exist between no other two people on this planet" (Ogden, 2009, p. 2).

The Hakomi method, too, especially its late "refined" version, addresses mental qualities reminiscent of those that interested Freud, Bion, and Winnicott and that still interest Ogden and not a few others. It focuses attention on these mental qualities as an indispensable basis for creating an appropriate therapeutic and interpersonal ground for the study of the psyche, and it aims to develop them first in the therapist and, through her, in the person seeking help: both through absorption, by the mere power of communication and time spent together, as well as directly, consciously and intentionally. A discourse concerning non-selective attention, dwelling in not-knowing and contact with the unknowable truth, about a mental space that enables the emerging mental contents to change and form by themselves, about states of immersion, and about the uniqueness and immediacy of the moment – such a discourse of necessity touches on qualities of attention and experiential processing that can be denoted "meditative". Still, this should not imply that therapeutic approaches that build on such a discourse actually employ meditation techniques in order to nurture these qualities.

What is learned today, in various versions, in various frameworks (universities, private study groups, schools, psychiatric hospitals, evening lectures in bars) and for various purposes (anxiety and stress management, treatment of depression and personality disorders, business success, spiritual search, enhancement of pupils' concentration and classroom climate), links the two senses of the word *mindfulness* and offers practical and easily implemented techniques that almost anyone can use almost anywhere. In a way, that's fine: these things are often done by good people with positive intentions and achieve good results. But in order to produce techniques that suit (nearly) everyone, in (nearly) every place, for so many different purposes, the techniques have had to be isolated from the context in which they came into being – the Buddha's path. One element of the path has had to be detached from the rest with which it was interwoven: from the world view, the insights and values in which it is supposed to be embedded and on which it is supposed to rest. It seems, sometimes, as if a whole doctrine – deep and far-reaching – was taken up and a few limited, custom-made derivations were removed from it, which now flutter, unconnected and confetti-like, in our cultural space.

Adages like "Be in the moment" or "As long as you live in the present moment, you won't have any problems", when shorn of an understanding of the nature of suffering, may be frustrating and discouraging for those whose "present moment" tends to be full of agony and confusion. Any talk about love and compassion remains hollow and detached until it also extends to a thorough investigation of the residues of hatred, ill will, and egoism that churn deep in the mind, dictating its actions in ways that remain neglected, unrecognized, outside the light of consciousness. Systematic attention (meditation) to breathing and body sensations takes an unexpected turn – instrumental, utilitarian, almost cynical, perhaps – when it abandons its roots to be recruited for the sake of narcissistic or material gains. In other cases, letting slip its transformative and ethical qualities, it becomes a superficial tranquilizer. Sometimes superficial and partial deployments are all a certain person in a certain situation can deal with; however, this may come at a price which is worth considering.

Being aware of something means developing a sensitivity to it. If this sensitivity is to be healthy, serving the mind for the purpose of growth and liberation, it must be accompanied by its complement: equanimity, or mental balance. Mental balance, in turn, requires a context of understanding and behavior if it is to have a chance to come about in the proper way. Hence, when the aim is to develop awareness in a systematic manner, this should occur along with a broader basis referring to "how", "why", and "for what purpose". Buddhist teaching offers this platform, and where training in systematic attentiveness is, as it were, removed from it and used in isolation, it is worth checking what is offered instead.

To gauge the general and long-term consequences of such a disjuncture may be difficult. The immediate personal outcomes are more easily observed, and further action should be considered, for each person specifically, in the light of these.

To conclude, as regards the first use of the term *mindfulness* – the universal state of mind or mental quality – an abundance of opportunities to practice it is always for the better, I believe. This is even more true with regard to the therapeutic domain. The therapist cannot be a beneficial presence if she doesn't at least seek to be aware of what goes on inside herself. This was a point well taken already by the first to occupy the psychotherapist's seat:

> We have noticed that no psycho-analyst goes further than his own complexes and internal resistances permit; and we consequently require that he shall begin his activity with a self-analysis and continually carry it deeper while he is making his observations on his patients. Anyone who fails to produce results in a self-analysis of this kind may at once give up any idea of being able to treat patients by analysis.
>
> (Freud, 1910, p. 145)

But when it comes to "mindfulness" in the more specific sense, touching upon techniques of training in systematic and continuous application of attention to an object of meditation, we may do well to consider the conditions, the tools, and the contexts in which they are learned.

Some reflections on the attitude to truth

Psychoanalytic discourse links sensitivity with truth and often ties them to injury, endless pain, and catastrophe. The Buddha's discourse asserts that suffering is a characteristic of existence, marking recognition and investigation of it as one of the necessary points of departure for the development of wisdom. The way it suggests, however, gradually leads to a situation in which sensitivity no longer means mental pain, and (mental) vulnerability in the face of the forces of becoming and annihilation – which are actually experienced more and more fully – decreases and eventually ceases.

Eigen (2004), following Bion, wrote, "Truth is highly charged, explosive, and if used wrongly, can wreck life. But without it, the soul is dead. For Bion, there is an emotional nourishment that comes with seeking the truth about ourselves, albeit use of truth in a compassionate or hateful way makes all the difference" (p. 7). Moving away, for a moment, from the insights of Bion and Eigen, I consider the many times I've heard the following, familiar voice: "I'll speak my truth, and I'll go on speaking my truth, no matter who gets hurt". Well, I ask myself, what exactly is this "truth"? And what precisely happens to the notion of truth when we couple it with "my" – in other words, when we attach attachment to it and appropriation? That's a big question. And this, it seems to me, at least in part, is the answer: What happens is that the so-called truth comes to serve a narrow subjective perspective, splitting "me" from "you" and separating their interests. Blind to the infinity of lines between them, the infinity of physical and mental particles they continuously exchange, this perspective imagines one may do harm without being harmed, that it is possible to separate "good for me" from "good for you", truth from compassion. "Tough love", I next hear another familiar voice, and a bunch of ill-used Zen stories pass through my mind: murder and dismemberment in the service of enlightenment. So, this "truth" of his, this appropriated, dismembering, killing "truth", is actually an act of compassion. The other person needs to hear it – if she doesn't, then it's her problem. She'll just have to; it's for her own good. Another danger of a spirituality that floats without moral anchor, cut off from the roots of proper understanding.

Someone feels he knows something, a sense of knowing arises. Is this knowledge a liberating truth or a terrorist in disguise? His personality and his habitual tendencies join in defining his ability to distinguish between the two. Often, cultural context and conventions come along and tip the balance towards either confusion or clear vision.

Not every truth is easy to digest – sometimes it hurts. But when a truth is compassionate, what makes it so is not self-conviction; rather, it is the quality of the mind that produces it: awake to interconnectedness and not splitting. Pure, and not stained by ignorance, desire, and hate. From a Buddhist point of view, when the mind uses a truth in a violent or otherwise destructive manner – whether against itself or against another – then this truth loses its status as truth. Truth can most certainly break and destroy: it can break and destroy illusion – which is what it does. But when a certain truth is spat out in contempt, with aggression and hate, then it is not truth. Where there is hate, there is ignorance. Truth and sobriety can only bring about compassion and love.

What inhabits the mind is part of the present reality. If this is how it is at some specific moment, it is truthful and sober to say, "Now there is hate in me". In this sense, truth and hate can coexist; but only in this sense. Truth cannot attack, hurt, or be used for evil purposes. Whatever attacks or injures is something else: it is inward- and outward-directed violence, which takes the form of hate, envy, greed, and other destructive forces that accumulate and multiply in the mind each time, in its ignorance, it reacts with craving towards the pleasant and with aversion towards the unpleasant.

Notes

1 The eightfold path is divided into three parts: wisdom (right view and right thought), morality (right speech, right bodily action, and right livelihood), and right concentration (right effort, right awareness or mindfulness, and right concentration).
2 *Sammā* – in the right manner, thoroughly, as should be, and in some contexts: in the best possible way, perfect.
3 Right speech (*sammā-vacā*), right bodily action (*sammā-kammanto*), and right livelihood (*sammā-ājīvo*).
4 Formally, this part of the path is called "right concentration". It includes right effort (*sammā-vāyāmo*), right mindfulness (*sammā-sati*), and right concentration (*sammā-samādhi*).
5 That is, *vipassanā* or *paññā*; as regards the parts of the way: right view (*sammā-diṭṭhi*) and right thought (*sammā-saṅkappo*).
6 Deep mental equanimity does not neglect the level of sensations. I will return to this in the next chapter.
7 Naturally, there are various interpretations and definitions. I follow this line of thought, as my teacher S. N. Goenka suggests and as I find clear and helpful.
8 Pāli is the language in which the Buddha's teachings (that is, early Buddhist text) were written.
9 Also, in other, more specific contexts: *jhāna* and *samādhi*.
10 Bion attributed this idea to Freud (Grotstein, 2000), but if we consider the passage he quotes for this purpose, he seems to have added or at least refined something. Here is the relevant quote:

> I know that in writing I have to blind myself artificially in order to focus all the light on one dark spot, renouncing cohesion, harmony, rhetoric and everything which you call symbolic, frightened as I am by the experience that any such claim or expectation involves the danger of distorting the matter under investigation, even though it may embellish it.
>
> (Freud, 1916)

References

Barnea-Astrog, M. (2017). *Carved by Experience: Vipassana, Psychoanalysis, and the Mind Investigating Itself*. London: Karnac.
Bion, W. R. (1962). *Learning from Experience*. London: Tavistock.
Bion, W. R. (1970). *Attention and Interpretation*. London: Tavistock.
Bion, W. R. (1988). Notes on memory and desire. In: E. B. Spillius (Ed.), *Melanie Klein Today (Vol. 2): Mainly Practice* (pp. 15–18). London: Routledge.

Dhp 1–2.

Eigen, M. (2004). *The Sensitive Self.* Middletown, CT: Wesleyan University.

Freud, S. (1908). Creative writers and day-dreaming. *S. E., 9*: 141–153, London: Hogarth, 1959.

Freud, S. (1910). The future prospects of psycho-analytic therapy. *S.E., 11*: 139–152. London: Hogarth.

Freud, S. (1912). Recommendations to physicians practising psycho-analysis, *S.E., 12*: 109–120.

Freud, S. (1916). Letter from Freud to Lou Andreas-Salomé, May 25, 1916. *International Psycho-Analytical Library, 89*: 45.

Freud, S. (1920). Beyond the pleasure principle. *S.E., 18*: 1–64.

Grotstein, J. S. (2000). Notes on Bion's "Memory and Desire". *Journal of American Academy of Psychoanalysis, 28*: 687–694.

Ogden, T. H. (2009). *Rediscovering Psychoanalysis: Thinking and Dreaming, Learning and Forgetting.* Hove: Routledge.

Payutto, P. A. (1995). *Dependent Origination: The Buddhist Law of Conditionality.* Translated by Bruce Evans. Thailand: Buddhadhamma Foundation.

Pelled, E. (2005). *Psychoanalysis and Buddhism: On the Human Capacity to Know.* Tel Aviv: Resling.

Winnicott, D. W. (1975). Primary maternal preoccupation. In: *Through Paediatrics to Psycho-Analysis* (pp. 300–305). London: Hogarth & the Institute of Psycho-Analysis.

Winnicott, D. W. (1987). *Babies and Their Mothers.* Cambridge: Perseus.

Chapter 3

Between pain and pleasure.

Khaṇasutta: the opportunity

You are fortunate, monks, so very fortunate, to have obtained the opportunity to live the holy life. Monks, I have seen a hell named "Six Spheres of Contact". There, whatever form one sees with the eye is undesirable, never desirable; displeasing, never pleasing; disagreeable, never agreeable. Whatever sound one hears with the ear is undesirable, never desirable; displeasing, never pleasing; disagreeable, never agreeable. Whatever odor one smells with the nose is undesirable, never desirable; displeasing, never pleasing; disagreeable, never agreeable. Whatever flavor one tastes with the tongue is undesirable, never desirable; displeasing, never pleasing; disagreeable, never agreeable. Whatever tactile object one touches with the body is undesirable, never desirable; displeasing, never pleasing; disagreeable, never agreeable. Whatever mental content one cognizes with the mind is undesirable, never desirable; displeasing, never pleasing; disagreeable, never agreeable.

You are fortunate, monks, so very fortunate, to have obtained the opportunity to live the holy life. Monks, I have seen a heaven named "Six Spheres of Contact". There, whatever form one sees with the eye is desirable, never undesirable; pleasing, never displeasing; agreeable, never disagreeable. Whatever sound one hears with the ear is desirable, never undesirable; pleasing, never displeasing; agreeable, never disagreeable. Whatever odor one smells with the nose is desirable, never undesirable; pleasing, never displeasing; agreeable, never disagreeable. Whatever flavor one tastes with the tongue is desirable, never undesirable; pleasing, never displeasing; agreeable, never disagreeable. Whatever tactile object one touches with the body is desirable, never undesirable; pleasing, never displeasing; agreeable, never disagreeable. Whatever mental content one cognizes with the mind is desirable, never undesirable; pleasing, never displeasing; agreeable, never disagreeable.

You are fortunate, monks, so very fortunate, to have obtained the opportunity to live the holy life.

–(SN 35.135)

One moment after another, we come into contact with the world; it is in the nature of our very being. And wherever contact is made, sensation arises. Shape, sound, smell, taste, and touch, image and emotion, memory and thought: the beautiful is pleasant and attractive, the ugly grates and makes one flinch. Our sensitivity is first of all sensuous, and each event, physical and mental, is accompanied by a sensation (AN 10.58). In a sense, it is the pleasure and the pain we experience, and the manner in which we perceive and react to them, that shape our life. This is the subject of this chapter: pain and pleasure as the bedrock of experience.

There are thirty-one planes of existence, according to Buddhist cosmology; thirty-one modes of existence in which the individual – human or otherwise – can be born, according to the residues of his actions – physical, vocal, and mental. Among these planes ours, that of humans, is extraordinary (SN 56.48), rare and precious. It is so precious because it consists of a special mixture of pain and pleasure (SN 35.135); and in terms of the road that leads from the coarse to the subtle, the chance to experience both is nothing less than the chance to experience the entire field of mind and matter and traverse it. Beings on the highest planes are purely mental, and as they lack both body and senses,[1] they are unable to feel bodily sensations, whether pleasant or unpleasant – which is a necessary condition for full liberation (Goenka, 1990). Beings from other high planes enjoy different kinds of bliss and delight; some are radiant, and some live in the air, free of difficulties. I can only imagine that in many cases[2] their motivation to change their condition must be much lower than ours. Those who exist in lower realms than our own are in permanent struggle with each other, or they endlessly and in vain pursue sensual pleasures that elude them, or again they are tortured by different kinds of pain. Their minds, in any case, are much less ready than ours to develop and improve. All of these conditions – pleasant or painful – are impermanent. The heavenly realms, from the Buddhist point of view, are not some eternal paradise, a desirable destination to reach, and dwelling in them is not some reward given by a supreme court. Existence in infernal realms, similarly, is not a form of punishment meted out by some external power, and it, too, will not go on forever. Every product of every action eventually exhausts itself, and even the incorporeal, the ones who lack concerns, those who dwell in bliss, and those who perhaps don't sense pain – neither will they remain in this state forever. This is why the Buddha's teachings look to stop the process of becoming, to achieve absolute release from endless wanderings between the thirty-one realms, infernal or heavenly as they may be. When this is the goal, the human condition is precious and unique.

Pleasure has a function. Pain has a function. There's a point to having the ability to experience each. They present us with an inclusive perspective, urge us towards liberation, and offer us the possibility to start on the way leading towards it.

How much pain, then, is necessary to get us to act towards liberation? When and in what circumstances will pain be an obstacle, complicating the process or delaying it? How much pleasure – and of what type – does it take for the mind to develop in a healthy manner, so it builds the necessary strength for further growth? When and in what circumstances does pleasure distract, conceal, or block? I have no intention to answer these questions in a methodical, comprehensive way, since the processes are incredibly complex and specific. Countless factors join in order to produce one moment in the life of one person, not to mention the processes of change or development or decline she goes through on her way from suffering to suffering or from suffering to release. Still, since I find thinking in terms of the functions of pain and pleasure useful, I will suggest some ideas that may nourish this thought by way of a starting point. I begin my examination from the psychodynamic aspect of the issue and continue with the Buddhist one, into which, then, the psychological basis will flow.

The mind's substrate

Freud saw mental life as channeled by two main principles: the pleasure principle and the reality principle. The pleasure principle is responsible for the intent to achieve pleasure and avoid displeasure. The reality principle enables one to take into account reality's strictures and – where necessary – to delay pleasure-seeking behaviors or to adjust them to the relevant conditions. It, too, however, is subject to the pleasure principle and bound to serve it (Freud, 1911). The only activities Freud identified as independent of the pleasure principle are the outcome of the repetition compulsion, which expresses the psychic principle of the death instinct (and only rarely appears in its pure form, unsupplemented by other motives that do come under the pleasure principle), and repetitive activities that take over in the acute event of trauma, when the system must regain control over the flood of stimuli and hence needs to put behaviors driven by the pleasure principle on hold for a while (Freud, 1920). These activities do not, of course, represent something that transcends the pleasure principle or is in some other sense free of it (Barnea-Astrog, 2017), but rather something whose function is even "more primitive, more elementary, more instinctual than the pleasure principle which it

over-rides" (Freud, 1920, p. 23). All there is beyond the pleasure principle is, in this view, action that enters the picture in emergencies, just until
basic order is restored and the system can once more seek pleasure and
continue to use reality for gratification. And underneath it all, perhaps,
as a basic characteristic of all instincts – the tendency towards total discharge, towards the annihilation of all excitation, a tendency directing
the system back to its original, inorganic state (Freud, 1920; Lazar &
Erlich, 1996). Therefore, while the complexity of the matter is fully
revealed when we consider the dynamic between the death instincts and
the life instincts – between ego-maintaining forces and those that drive
reproduction and development, and between these and the repetition
compulsion and the drive to non-existence – we find that for Freud, the
pleasure principle usually holds sway.

Bion added a third principle to the pleasure and reality principles: the
truth principle (Pelled, 2005). He believed that, just like the body needs
food, the mind needs truth. Truth enables growth, and contact with it
depends on the ability to tolerate displeasure and frustration. In Bion's
theory, the sphere of human mental activity can extend beyond the pleasure principle – truly beyond it, and not just at its feet. We can therefore
spot the difference: while for Freud the function of thinking is to reduce
tension, to participate in processes that remove pain and frustration, and
to attain satisfaction, for Bion thinking comes to manage and regulate
tension, participate in processes that allow us to tolerate pain and frustration, and serve the truth (Symington & Symington, 1996). Given a sufficient ability to tolerate frustration, absence of the satisfying object can
transform into thought within the mind[3] – an idea of "breast missing" –
and a system for thinking evolves (Bion, 1962b). Hence, thinking allows
managing frustration, while the ability to handle frustration enhances the
development of thought. If, by contrast, the ability to bear frustration is
slim, the mind will seek to evade frustration by means of voiding itself
of the intolerable elements.

Bion explained the development of the ability to think and to tolerate the unpleasant by means of a model of container and contained. The
immature psyche, according to this model, is in need of a proper container
(sufficiently open and supple) so as to project into it what it cannot bear
itself. Inside this container – which is not static and not even a "thing"
(Bion, 1962a), but rather a process (Ogden, 2004) – intolerable mental
contents are digested or metabolized, then to be returned in a more useful state to the one who projected them. By means of this process, what
was too terrible and raw to be thought becomes meaningful. Where the
parental container is functional, the infant will eventually internalize this

containing-digesting function following many rounds of the metabolic dynamic. It will be available to her for coping with the internal and external reality, and she will be able to think or dream it; that is, to be in contact with it, to grow as a result of this connection. When the container is dysfunctional – blocked, leaking, refusing entrance to difficult materials, or unable to deal with them in a healthy manner – the infant might internalize a "negative container" or an "obstructive object" (Grotstein, 1995). In such a case, or when the infant's projections are excessive or her internalizing capacity is somehow impaired, there is a great danger for the process to fail and for her ability to perceive and digest reality to be damaged (Bion, 1959, 1962b) and that, instead of taking back in what has become usable, meaning-generating mental substance, she will experience raw, insufferable experiences such as "nameless dread" (Bion, 1962a, p. 309). Consequently, it is quite possible that her contact with truth and her ability to learn from experience will be negatively affected, that she will be further imprisoned by the need to gain satisfaction and to void herself of discontent, and that the pleasant experiences she is able to have will be tainted or distorted as well.

The good object

The container-contained model is, among other things, an elaboration of Klein's ideas about introjection, projection, and projective identification. Klein described how the psyche, while interrelating with its objects, is molded through a complex dynamic between introjection and projection (1946, 1975a). In simplified terms, this process consists of the infant absorbing or ingesting the world, projecting onto it her internal contents and experiences, then re-introjecting them once they have blended with the perceived extraneous characteristics. This is how she constitutes herself: through introjecting the world. This is how she absorbs the world: painted in her own hues. This is how she experiences herself: through the re-introjection of her own contents after they have become fused with the features of the world.

What exactly does she project? What does she take back in? Living in a realm of existence that involves both suffering and pain, the baby has pleasant and difficult experiences. The pleasant ones are related to satisfying nursing, soothing, and love. The hard ones are linked to frustration, pain, and a whole lot of primitive anxieties triggered and amplified by them. Klein argues that the infant, to fend off these anxieties and especially a sense of internal destructiveness associated with the death instinct, separates or "splits" (unconsciously and in fantasy) her world's "good" elements, which gratify, soothe pain, and give pleasure, from the "bad" ones, which frustrate, don't soothe pain, and don't provide pleasure. In parallel, she splits (unconsciously and in fantasy) the "good" elements inside herself – the loving and loved parts – from the "bad" elements, which hate and are hated. Splitting helps her produce an illusive sense of order. She feels as though the good things dwell together, a safe long way from anything bad. The archetype of the good is the available and nourishing breast; the archetype of evil is the absent breast that fails to nourish. Therefore, if in reality there is a breast which is available and nourishing at times and then again absent or empty; there is a mother (or father) who is sometimes present, her face loving and attentive, and at other times either absent, or her expression angry, anxious, or set; and there is an infantile psyche, which now experiences tenderness and love and next hate and anger surge up in it – then following the way the early psyche works, a good breast and a bad breast emerge, a good mother or father and a bad mother or father, and loving self-parts that exist separately from hating self-parts.

Splitting relieves anxiety while creating a "good breast" or a "good object", an element which, if it is internalized through feelings of satisfaction and love, will be perceived as unblemished. Once it is in place it will encourage the further internalization of good objects and situations, which then will further allay anxiety, and so on (Klein, 1975a). The good object is a vital component in the construction of the self. So, while extreme splitting and projection will impoverish the self, weaken it, and cause pathology (Klein, 1946), normal splitting and projection are necessary parts of early, healthy development. Without them there is no conservation of the good object, whose introjection is required for consolidation and the development of the ability to love (Klein, 1975b).

According to Alvarez (2012), this important aspect of Klein's theory was somewhat neglected in Bion's clinical and theoretical developments. Alvarez took issue with Freud and Bion, who saw impeding and unpleasant forces like absence, frustration, and separation as the main or primary contributors in the emergence of reality and thinking. She suggested that the process by which thought becomes thinkable also occurs in the context of a living presence and when its object is joyful and pleasurable. Alvarez believed psychoanalysis tends to present pleasurable situations as passive, symbiotic, somnolent, and mindless and argued for pleasure-giving experiences as having an activating potential, accompanied by, and in turn stimulating, thought. She thus underlined the importance, alongside frustration and coping with it – something which has been copiously discussed – of paying attention to experiences of pleasure, security, and delight as necessary to emotional health. The alpha function, she said, aims not only to digest absence and whatever is experienced as insufferable; it also "operates on present and pleasurable objects" (p. 77).

Alvarez's stress on "the texture, feel, sound and look of a kind or good object" (p. 77) indicates how important positive experiences are for growth and learning. Klein's notion of the "good object" suggests the need for some body of goodness, experienced as unblemished; a body that is the outcome of pleasant-benign-nourishing experiences registered by the mind-body system in the wake of a loving, satisfying encounter with one's environment.

A good environment

A good-enough environment, said Winnicott (1975), allows the infant to experience the satisfactions, anxieties, and conflicts appropriate to her stage of development. This environment, to a large extent, takes the shape of her mother (or the main caregiver), who succeeds in delicately and sensitively adapting herself to the infant's needs (p. 302). This is what Winnicott wrote about the nature of these needs and the mother's or caregiver's attitude to them:

> You will understand I am not simply referring to her being able to know whether the baby is or is not hungry, and all that sort of thing; I am referring to innumerable subtle things, things that only my friend the poet could properly put into words. For my part, I am contented to use the word *hold*, and to extend its meaning to cover all that a mother is and does at this time [the first few weeks of the baby's life]. [. . .] It is here that she cannot learn from books. She cannot use even Spock just at this point where she feels that the baby needs to be picked up, or put down, to be left alone or to be turned over, or where she knows that what is essential is the simplest of all experiences, that based on contact without activity, where there is opportunity for the feeling of oneness between two persons who are in fact two and not one. These things give the baby the opportunity to be, out of which there can arise the next things that have to do with action, doing and being done to. Here is the basis for what gradually becomes, for the infant, the self-experiencing being.
>
> (Winnicott, 1987, pp. 6–7)

Let's consider a parent who is holding a baby in the first weeks of his life. He will hold the infant's limbs in such a way that they won't dangle loosely, every which way – so that the infant, who is as yet unable to hold himself, can feel safe. More than anything, he will hold the baby's head so it won't flop. Good-enough holding supports a (primitive, raw) sense of self as uniform and smooth, which can be thought of as a circle. Bad holding ruptures this unconscious ongoing line and forces the baby to grow prematurely aware of his sense of self: body and head, two circles that have become detached (Winnicott, 1987). If, in the first stages of the baby's life, the mother is able to invest herself in caring for him, in a specific psychological state Winnicott (1975) called "primary maternal preoccupation", to "hold" the baby properly – physically and mentally – and to offer him a good-enough environment that adjusts itself to his needs – then she supports the natural unfolding of his characteristics and tendencies and their expressions, and she allows him to "experience spontaneous movement and become the owner of the sensations that are appropriate to this early stage of life" (ibid., p. 303). If she fails, then the infant's "line of life" (ibid.) is disturbed by his reactions to impingements, something that unsettles his sense of "going-on-being" (ibid.). Such disturbances are nothing less than the threat of annihilation (ibid.), and a whole spectrum of primitive agonies (Winnicott, 1974) might come along.

For Winnicott, the constitution of self is based in the experience of continuity, the experience of "going-on-being". When this experience is sufficiently established, the infant's relations with the mother, who gradually becomes a human being in his perception, can start to emerge, and his ability to control his urges and to handle frustration and difficulty begins to be built (ibid.). Once again we witness how the assimilation of goodness is the basis of the ability to connect (with the other, with reality) and the ability to bear the harsh and unpleasant.

Here it needs to be mentioned that although the pair "need" and "response to need" and the pair "frustration" and "satisfaction" (of desire or lust) are interlinked, they must be distinguished. This is how Winnicott did it:

> Incidentally I feel that the introduction of the word "need" instead of "desire" has been very important in our theorizing, but I wish Miss Freud had not used the words "satisfaction" and "frustration" here; a need is either met or not met, and the effect is not the same as that of satisfaction and frustration of id impulse. [. . .] it would be a distortion to say that the infant who is not lulled reacts as to a

frustration. Certainly there is not anger so much as some kind of distortion of development at an early phase.

(Winnicott, 1975, p. 301)

The needs Winnicott referred to are natural, healthy, developmentally appropriate, legitimate, inherent ones. When they are perceived as such and seen as distinct from instinctual desires (which, too, may be natural, developmentally appropriate, legitimate, and inherent, though in a different way), this supports a surrendering – rather than an antagonistic – state of mind that neither judges the infant's needs nor fights them. For Winnicott, this state, first of all, is what "primary maternal preoccupation" is about. But he formulates a position which also encourages the gentle holding of the adult person – some of whose primitive mental layers did not get a good-enough response, and therefore remained alive and active and continue affecting her life in ways that cause suffering.

Balint too discussed basic favorable conditions, natural goodness – the need for which is inherent – and the distortion that arises when they are absent. Goodness, as he described it, is associated with a kind of primary love, with a well-adjusted, understanding, and undemanding environment which the infant (and later, the patient) "should be in no way obliged to take notice, to acknowledge, or to be concerned about" (Balint, 1968, p. 180). Safe, unobtrusive, quiet, and harmonious, this environment allows the infant to peacefully love. Balint used the notion of the "basic fault" to denote the distortion resulting from the opposite condition: its roots, as well as its healing, are distinct from the domain of the instincts. Balint's "fault" is not a state, a position, a complex or a conflict. It is experienced as "something wrong in the mind" or as something missing, "a kind of deficiency that must be put right" (Balint, 1968, p. 21). This fault's impact extends throughout the psycho-biological structure. It originates in an excessive gap between a person's mental and physical needs early in life and the psychological and material caring she received. Such a discrepancy can be caused by inborn factors due to which the child's needs are uncommonly demanding, but it can equally be the result of environmental factors, or in other words, caring that for some reason or another failed. Either way, the basic fault, even though it is dynamic, does not originate in a biological drive or in conflict. It is not an obstruction in need of release; nor can it be satisfied, as would be the case with an instinctual need, or settled, as in the case of a conflict. Perhaps it can be healed "provided the deficient ingredients can be found; and even then it may amount only to a healing with defect, like a simple, painless scar" (Balint, 1968, p. 22).

Nourishment

Winnicott described the good-enough environment and good-enough holding that enables a round, smooth, and continuous experience, as well as the catastrophe that occurs when this experience is prematurely disrupted. Balint described an understanding and harmonious environment that enables the infant to quietly love and simply to be, as well as the basic fault that cracks the psyche when the caring environment isn't experienced as such. Both suggest the mind-body system's basic need of a primal experience of smoothness, sweetness, and harmony. Prior to being able to tolerate anything else, the emergent self needs a sufficient dose of this feeling in order to develop in a healthy manner. This isn't a luxury. Kurtz, who created the Hakomi method, called this necessary, natural, legitimate, inherent goodness "nourishment" (Kurtz, Martin, & Sparks, 2013). While the archetypal food for the body is mother's milk, the archetypal mental nourishment is what the infant feels as she nurses. When everything functions as it should, these are pleasant physical and mental sensations. This pleasantness is linked with soothing and sweetness, and it occurs as part of a relationship – between two people – even if the self of one of them is still at very early stages of emergence. It is the pleasantness of satisfaction that precedes instinctual desire and of contentedness that comes before will. (From a Buddhist perspective, features of desire and will are bound up with any creature – no matter how primitive – as long as it moves through the cycle of becoming and dying. In the present context I am thinking of instinctual desire and will of the kind that presumes the existence of a psychological self in the full sense; psychoanalytic thinkers hold various views regarding the existence of a self from the outset of life).

Qualities similar to those characteristic of successful breastfeeding also occur in other nourishment-related situations, and in this sense nourishment can be considered "psychological nursing" (Balint, 1968, p. 186). Here the nourishment is made up of the joint experiences covered under "good-enough holding" and "a favorable environment". They are simple – undistorted, that is – experiences of *being*. They can be detailed in a long list of experiences which the subjective entity expects: when she is in her diapers and unable as yet to mentalize them, much like when she's fully developed – if we can ever use an expression of this sort.

It is easy to see how the feeling that there is someone who sees, attends, adjusts herself; who provides time and space; has a steady, uninvasive, unimposing presence; with whom one may experience a plethora of feelings and positions without the threat of disintegration of either self or other; who offers something to hold onto but also allows letting go; and so forth – that this feeling is linked with the above-mentioned qualities. When at the start of life, a certain nourishing experience, or a cluster of such experiences, is insufficiently available, then the body-mind system organizes itself in order to cope with this absence and to avoid, as much as possible, the associated pain. Though this way of coping, like any other attempt to come to terms with early lack, has its appreciable survival and adaptive value, it comes at a price. One such price is that this type of organization causes the individual to stop recognizing the missing nourishing experiences, even when, later on, they may be available; it thus deletes them from the repertoire of accessible experiences – those perceived as possible – and this perpetuates the lack.

If a person learns early in life that there is no responsible adult looking after him, then he may develop an always-responsible part that stays vigilant, day and night. It will be impossible for him to fully relax or be totally immersed in some pleasurable activity. If a woman learns that there is no one to hold her, then it is likely that something inside her will ensure that she holds herself. She will find it hard or impossible to let go and experience the nourishment that is the result of external holding, even in relationships that might have offered this. If another woman has learned, at the start of her life, that there is no one to regulate her, then something within her is likely to learn how to do it herself – maybe by making sure that she will not even begin to develop any emotion that is too hard to manage. Contact with more considerable emotional intensities, as well as the option to put an end to the ongoing labor of regulation, will be alien to her, outside the range of possibility. If another person grew up in an intrusive environment, he might evolve ways of detaching and sealing himself, which would then be in the way of making contact with himself and others. It is a good thing that these people learned to look after themselves, to hold themselves, to do their own regulation and keep themselves away from harmful factors, or else the outcome would be much more destructive. But something fundamentally nourishing will be beyond their reach, and the physical and mental effort demanded by these adaptive organizations is heavy and continuous, entrenching discontent while masking or distorting traits that are not permitted to thrive and flourish.

Holding a gentle baby

For the parent of a gentle baby, generating a holding and well-attuned environment is not likely to be a simple job. All babies are sensitive to facial expression, tone of voice, and other gestures of people in their surroundings, especially their parents. All babies are sensitive to how they are being held and handled, to heat and cold, to pain and hunger, to motion and position, to the air outside and the ambience indoors, to sadness and joy, indifference and love. When we grow up, still, we continue reacting automatically and unconsciously to the nonverbal communication of the people surrounding us and to the conditions of our environment, as they make contact with our subjective constitution and trigger sensations. In this sense, we are all sensitive. Yet there are some for whom this process takes a different place, more frontal, and with a somewhat different resolution.

Gentleness is associated with subtlety, and the gentle person registers subtleties and reacts to them. The merest change in external conditions affects her. The smallest shift in internal circumstances affects her. What may be good enough for one infant may not do at all for the gentle infant. The task of adjustment and responding to needs is more complex in this sense for parents of such children: at times they ask for degrees of attention and accuracy that are not equally developed in all of us. On the other side of the interaction, that of the baby, incompatibility is likely to be experienced as a harsh jarring, and often she cannot pass this unnoticed. And so, her feedback to the parent's inability (momentary or ongoing) to attune and respond will be loud and clear. If there are not enough other opportunities in which their interactions result in calmness, restfulness, quiet, attentive activity, and content, the parent may eventually take the baby's expressions as blame: "Failure! Failure! Failure!" In such a case, the parent's confidence is likely to suffer, and along with it his naturalness, his clarity, and his ability to hold and contain. These, in turn, will have their effect on the shaping of the baby's mental life and parent–infant relations.

Other than manifestations of anxiety, restlessness (both mental and physical) and loneliness, another possible product of this dynamic is confusion. When a woman experiences reality at a higher resolution than the people around her – including those who are responsible for her care – her clarity regarding her perception of external and internal reality may well become troubled. One could say that she sees and perceives what the others don't see and perceive. A subtle transmission that lands on grosser receptors (wholly normal, often, but in this case relatively blunt) is not fully – or perhaps fully not – absorbed. Here, the ones whose receptors they are cannot receive the transmission and come up with an appropriate response. If this happens regularly, the transmission starts to become distorted. Each and every one of us experiences reality in a specific and unique way, and a certain discrepancy between what we transmit and what others receive is only to be expected. But when this discrepancy is more extensive – as often is the case with gentle or very sensitive people – the experience is more deeply engraved.

Louise: a choreography of nuances

Of the several narratives that come to my mind in this context, Louise's is one that touched me especially. I have known her for a number of years. She is a pleasant-looking woman of around fifty, a physiotherapist and dancer who started as a student of mine and then became a supervisee. Early on in our acquaintance it was obvious that she was a person who looked deeply into things, who weighed up matters inquiringly, not letting nuances go unnoticed. Another thing that stood out was a troubled tone, a kind of restlessness: not of the fidgety type, but in a way, rather heavyhearted, and a confusion that appeared as a layer of doubt and blurriness that would at times take over and replace her ability to see.

This confusion was repeatedly manifest in the course of the years of our meetings. It could take different shapes: It accompanied her intellectual processes and would get in the way of putting order to the many experiential details she perceived – in herself and in others – making it impossible to identify the direction into which she would like to move. It would blur her ability to feel what was right for her, thereby maintaining and fueling discontent. When she was in her role as therapist it would at times descend on her like a screen and paralyze her. My feeling was that her confusion occurred alongside, or on top of, her sharp perception and wisdom rather than in their place – but the layer of bewilderment this produced infused her with doubt and an almost constant strain. Working with this as we did with all the other materials that emerged, it accumulated meaning and began to dissolve as time went by.

I remember one distinct moment in this process, which occurred in a small supervision group. This type of group usually includes four or five participants who have been studying the Hakomi method for at least three years. Each time one of the participants is in the role of the therapist, another takes that of the person who studies himself, and the remainder, called "assistants", help create the right space and support the process in different ways. Bodily expressions are often extremely present in the meeting, requiring simple touch for the sake of holding and in service of the investigation (see, for example, Barnea-Astrog, 2015). Unlike the more regular, one-to-one therapeutic situation, in which I avoid physical contact since I believe it to be safer, the skilled small group allows us to lean on the assistants for this purpose. The instructor – me, in this case – attends the event and offers the therapist advice in real time.

Let's return to Louise. On this occasion she was in the role of the person who studied herself (the patient), and she immediately reported discomfort and restlessness, physical and mental. She tried to find a way to relax a little. She tried to sit in one way and then in another. To lean or not lean. To lie down. She lay on her back and then turned on her side. She bent her knees and held them together. Rolled over to the other side. She tried to find the right place to put her head, her arms, her legs, her neck. As she was looking inward, aware of what was happening there, we tried to support her with a pillow, a headrest, a wall, or a hand. We tried to hold the tense, cramped areas on her face, her skull, shoulders, knees, back – without any attempt to suppress the discomfort, to resolve or fix it; we tried to stay with her sensitively and with sympathetic curiosity, responding as best we could. Every attempt Louise made led to a sense of impreciseness. Each and every position, however right it seemed to begin with, would rapidly turn inappropriate, impelling her to shift. Each time she just started to relax a little, another bout of restlessness arose, which then would be equally unappeasable. We found ourselves following her ever more closely, changing along with her from moment to moment, shifting with her in what gradually became a dance of adjustment, a choreography of nuances.

She spoke about a feeling that accompanied her in the various relationships she had had, a feeling that she was hard to be with. That she was not understood, that she was too complicated, a difficult person, a difficult patient. She was concerned for us, didn't want us to feel obliged to cope with her – wasn't that impossible anyway? She felt homeless, without a place in the world, detached. She knew yet didn't know what would be right for her, felt the irritation of incongruity yet couldn't manage to see beyond it – what might feel good, what might fit.

Clarity and confusion came and went, taking turns, blending together, clashing. In time Louise grew more curious about what was happening, as it gradually took on shape and meaning with us looking on. An association came up, perhaps an image, or perhaps a memory, of herself as a baby in the arms of her mother, who doesn't know where to put her or what to do with her. This image was forceful and clear, and it was attended by an experience she knew all too well: a feeling of deep and persistent discontent, a kind of mental and physical squirming that doesn't allow surrender to the here and now, that doesn't make it possible simply to be. She was a fifty-year-old woman with the wisdom of someone her age and more, but this infantile layer was alive in her, running her from within. She moved this way and that, not finding peace; she couldn't quite position herself, yearning for something that would settle her but that never properly arrived.

Like a parent to a baby who is hard to soothe, in this type of situation the therapist too may be drawn into a constellation marked by a sense of failure, frustration, anger, and guilt; she may well find herself caught up in anxiety and insecurity, or disconnecting and emotionally abandoning the patient. Like a parent – but also unlike her – she may feel tempted to try and repair, to quickly erase the discontent and replace it with a good feeling: like a parent because both can harbor a reparative impulse based on anxiety and difficulty tolerating unpleasantness, but unlike a parent because the balance between the space devoted to allowing discontent and staying with it and the space devoted to relief is different for a more competent, adult patient than for a baby – provided the aim is healthy processing. However that may be, realizing that it is the actual work of attention and adjustment that is the central process here is likely to contribute to the ability to not be carried away on a vortex of anger and guilt, by the anxious effort to repair or by detachment. The work of attention and adjustment is not expected to lead to absolute compatibility, to the perfect fit of glove to hand. It is, rather, the work of endeavor: lending a curious and sympathetic ear to the other, addressing one's will and gaze to the subterranean streams that are asking for just this. For the person studying himself, too, realizing that this is the crux of the matter gives meaning to the process. His view of unpleasantness and difficulty changes, turning them from something loathsome that he must be rid of into objects of investigation, interesting and precious in themselves.

In the case of Louise, the work of attention and adjustment was the central process because, for her, the experience most deeply engraved as missing was that of an observant maternal mind that perceived subtleties, acknowledged them and their right to exist, and was capable of responding to them – not at every single moment and not fully, but often enough and close enough to being full. The work of attention and adjustment was central in the sense that experiencing it in the therapeutic-learning space created the possibility for Louise to investigate the means she had developed in order to cope with the early lack, as well as the opportunity to experience – for brief moments that were gradually absorbed and expanded – what until then had been unthinkable. Now her subtle transmission met with subtle receptors that were able to properly perceive her and respond to her. And because this happened repeatedly and systematically over the course of a number of years, the earlier distortion began to disentangle. Once Louise was offered the opportunity to attend, again and again, to the nuances of the flow of her experience – the need, the discontent, the natural spring, the rhythm that sought expression – in a setting that was attuned to them, allowed them to pass through its *reverie* and held them with confidence and love, the confused state of mind lost its grounding and began to dissipate. In this space she found a home. Her discernment and accuracy no longer clashed with what had screened them, and slowly on they found more expression, softly glowing against the background of relative ease that started to emerge in both her body and her mind.

Necessary goodness and instinctual gratification

If expressions of need encounter well-adjusted hands and eyes, and hence don't become blurred or malformed, then they don't threaten the wholeness of the self. Surrounded by the goodness of attention and response, frustration becomes meaningful and tolerable. Surrounded by the lucidity they afford, discontent transforms into an object of investigation that is not entirely devoid of delight in itself.

Let us now return to Winnicott, who wrote:

In reconstructing the early development of an infant there is no point at all in talking of instincts, except on a basis of ego development.

There is a watershed:

Ego maturity – instinctual experiences strengthen ego.

Ego immaturity – instinctual experiences disrupt ego.

Ego here implies a summation of experience. The individual self starts as a summation of resting experience, spontaneous motility, and sensation, return from activity to rest, and the gradual establishment of a capacity to wait for recovery from annihilations; annihilations that result from reactions to environmental impingement.

(Winnicott, 1975, p. 305)

The self is an accumulation of experiences, and good experiences must be sufficiently dominant in order to constitute a self that has the strength to deal with the difficult experiences: tension, instinctual urge, frustration, lack. A reasonable amount of lack and frustration stimulates the hallucinatory fulfillment of wishes that is related to the ability to think – and anyway, it is inevitable. Furthermore, anxiety spurs development when it drives the person to cope and seek creative solutions (Durban & Roth, 2013). However, and to the same extent if not more, anxiety also endangers development as it attacks thinking processes and the ability to feel, to contain, and to hold (ibid.). And so, even if a gradual decrease in the degree of compatibility between the mother-environment and the infant is only natural and necessary, it has to occur in a manner and with a pace that suit the baby's developing abilities so that obliteration does not exceed recovery and anxiety does not too often cross the line between encouraging growth and endangering it.

If this is not the case, and things are too difficult early in life, then the unfavorable ratio between lack and nourishment may take root in the body-mind in a way that will make it hard for the psyche to develop qualities that will allow it, in due time, to set itself free from harmful habits; that is, from its own shackles. If it has not internalized a functional container, if it didn't develop a reasonable mental metabolism, then reality, internal as well as external, will be insufferable, and the mind will be pushed to void itself of itself,[4] even in adulthood. If it has not internalized a good object, its ability to consolidate and to love will be affected. If (due to external or internal conditions – or most likely due to misfit, or the meeting point of both) it has not had an adjusted-enough environment, a kind of "basic fault" might form in the psyche, which will undermine its ability to self-reflect (Balint, 1968). If the body-mind wasn't provided with good-enough holding, physical and mental, then compensatory holding mechanisms will come into play. The spontaneous movement of authentic expression might be disrupted, and its place will be taken by a "false self" (Winnicott, 2016), whose relation to the truth is intricate.

"Where there are no good memories and where thinking and memory are impaired, there is no healing", said Alvarez (2012, p. 77). Goodness is crucial, and by contrast, at least in the early stages of life, the more exposed a person is to traumatic experiences, the more disrupted the self's process of development (Alvarez, 2012; Epstein, 2015). Of course, as said, the emergence of conditions that stand in the psyche's way of developing growth-supporting qualities is not only a matter of the degree and nature of lack and discrepancy. It also depends on the way in which that particular psyche is able to handle these things. So many internal and external factors determine the extent of the psyche's ability to survive in good health what is experienced as disturbance, and to grow from it, that it is not possible to take full account of them. Some of them are connected in a circular manner with exactly the same processes which I have just mentioned: internalization of a good object, digestion and containment, holding and a compatible environment, the accumulation of nourishing experiences. All these are development-supporting conditions which then feed further development-supporting conditions. The seeds of some of these were sown at different points in time and space, even before the birth of the person in question, whose body and mind now have to deal with the consequences. (The latter can be considered as abstractions and extensions of the former; extensions that transcend the constraints of thinking about the specific history of an individual phenomenon. I will return to these further on in this chapter as well as in the final parts of this book.)

There is, therefore, a difference between "necessary goodness" and instinctual gratification. Necessary goodness is precisely that: it touches on the experiential matter crucial for building the psyche, whose positive forces outweigh the negative. Where the sense of goodness is more powerful than the sense of badness, suggested Alvarez (2012), this results in integrated, concerned, or caring states. Where the sense of goodness fails to outdo badness, paranoid and/or persecutory states emerge. Where both senses of good and of bad are feeble, states of emptiness and/or dissociation are the outcome. An elaboration on Klein's theory concerning the relations between the depressive and the paranoid-schizoid positions, this model underlines, in addition to the importance of experiencing both good and bad, that it is necessary for the good to hold sway. When this is the case, positive feelings like love, confidence, potency, self-worth, and a drive for reparation and justice take the upper hand over negative feelings such as hatred, fear, suspiciousness, shame, impotence, despair, and destructiveness (Alvarez, 2012).

A sufficient amount of pleasurable experiences of the first kind, therefore, nourishes the mind, offering it the conditions that support developmental achievements. The experience of pleasure of the second kind I will shortly discuss, when I consider the function of sensations as objects of sensual desire. Pleasant and unpleasant are just what they are: pleasant and unpleasant. But the mental attitude of the person who experiences them is different in these two contexts. While it isn't always easy to draw the line between them, the experiential fields that I am referring to here are defined so that the first (necessary goodness) constitutes the grounds for the ability to bear the unpleasant, to connect with reality, and to grow supported by truth; the second (instinctual gratification or satisfaction of id impulses), however, relates – at least from the Buddhist perspective – to reactive mental processes that fan desire and hate and get in the way of contact with the truth.

The adult mind

While sensitivity refers to the experience of "more" pain and pleasure, gentleness is about the attitude with which this pain and pleasure are attended. Where gentleness involves fragility and destructiveness, the attitude to pain and pleasure results in suffering. This attitude changes where gentleness is mature, representing a position of non-violence towards both self and other.

If a good object was fostered and internalized, if containment and holding were good enough, if the environment was reasonably attuned, if essential nourishing experiences were ingested by the system, if a relatively mature self with coping abilities developed (with the help of the environment, and at times in spite of it) – then we may start to talk about development and liberation of a different order, like those suggested in the Buddha's teachings. Here I have to add a reservation: In the broader context linear criteria do not entirely apply, and one cannot simply say, "First get healthy enough, and then only turn to setting yourself free". This is because we cannot be aware of all personal and environmental factors that are at play in each case, in order to bring them to bear in a way that will yield a formula. Alongside the personal biographical factors, there are always other factors of a different order, and we must not reduce our thinking to the specific confines of the individual or claim we can follow the ways that meander between acts and their fruits, between fruits and their seeds.

We should therefore hold, tenderly and cautiously, both ends of the rope: maintain a wide perspective while at the same time acknowledging that the path is long and that following it requires certain mental strengths (which develop and grow as one goes along). Deep meditation practice raises different layers of mental accumulations to the surface of the mind, and a minimal measure of stability is necessary to deal with them in a healthy manner. In specific cases, partial or superficial versions of meditation may also benefit those in more unstable, acute mental states (the Buddha himself gave different instructions to different people, according to their state, capacities, and inclinations); but in these cases, the domain of practice must be considerably limited, and careful, close, professional guidance should be provided. Vipassana practice as such, in its entirety and as it is offered to the public, is not meant for those suffering acute mental states, nor for those who suspect they might be on the verge of entering such a state.

Now, while avoiding getting stuck in the attempt to define it, I will revert to the psyche whose grounds – whenever it was made, whatever it was made of – allow it to start working towards liberation from its shackles. I will discuss how pleasantness and unpleasantness play a role in this.

From prince to ascetic

Siddhattha Gotama, later known as the Buddha, lived a very affluent and protected life. When he was born, son to King Suddhodana and Queen Maya (Māyā), the elders predicted one of two possible courses of life: either he would grow up to be a great ruler, a good and benevolent king, or he would renounce the life of a householder in order to take up the life of spiritual practice. In that case he would become a Buddha: a man awakened from all illusion, destined to reveal the wisdom that casts light on the nature of things and the way to absolute liberation from suffering, and to spread it for the good of all. Queen Maya died about a week after the birth of her son, and King Suddhodana, as might be expected from a dedicated father, wanted the boy to take the first course. He didn't want him to become an ascetic, wandering homeless in the world; he wanted him to raise a family and succeed him in due time. To ensure this would happen and to avoid the second possibility, he did everything to make his son's life safe and sumptuous. All his senses were to be indulged and placated, and anything that might cause him pain had to be removed. And so it happened that Siddhattha only saw an old person, a sick person, and a dead person after he grew up.[5] (Those with a western psychodynamic inclination will probably comment: But his mother died very shortly after he was born.)

Human existence entails pain, and pain is likely to arouse destructive feelings. Anger, despair, confusion, doubt, hate, envy, and grudges might cause the psyche to contract around its egocentric core and remove it from its brothers and sisters, the other sentient beings around it. Given the right mental grounds, the very same pain can become a "noble pain" – awakening the one who experiences it and urging him to examine the nature of reality, tying him to other living creatures whom he recognizes as fellow-sufferers, and instigating a process of liberation.

Pain can therefore form an obstacle to the mind's way to truth, but it can also fuel the pursuit of it. Pleasure, too, can offer a basis to connect with truth or function like a screen that occludes it. In the language of psychology, a basis of necessary goodness is a fundamental support for a person's ability to be in touch with internal and external reality and tolerate their inherent pain. For the future Buddha, this encounter between the basis of goodness and the reality of suffering was particularly dramatic.

Given the abundant life from which he was fortunate enough to start, and given his specific virtues, realizing the existence of pain – over and beyond being inevitable – turned out to be a precious catalyst.

Sickness, old age, and death presented themselves and struck him. Pain grated against pleasantness and ignited insight. Hardship met delicateness and prompted a process that had just been waiting to bear fruit. Pampered in luxury, beauty, and refinement, young Siddhattha realized that he too was fated to fall ill, grow old, and die. Every living being is bound to fall ill, grow old, and die. Suffering prevails, and no amount of pleasantness will cover it up. He decided to give up everything and seek the way to total liberation.

In the course of the six years after he left the palace and until he reached his destination, Siddhattha studied the most profound meditation techniques available with the best teachers that could be found. He, who was raised in plenty as befits a prince, chose to torture his body following one of the then-prevailing notions, which held that self-mortification was a necessary condition for obtaining release from the cause of suffering – desire. While reaching a very seriously run-down physical condition, he still identified vestiges of the same defilements that came between him and full liberation – the object of his entire effort. The way of self-mortification did not work.

So he abandoned this avenue, much to the amazement and contempt of the other ascetics with whom he had been practicing. Once he found what he had been looking for and succeeded in uprooting the last of his mind's defilements, he formulated one of the aspects of the "middle path", which passed between the two extremes that were known in the spirituality of his time: neither extreme deprivation and torture nor wallowing in the pleasures of the senses would set a person free, but a disciplined way of living that offers the body (and the mind) what they need in order to be healthy and persist in their work. There is no point in sentencing the body (and the mind) to sorrow by design. Nor is there a point in running incessantly after the satisfaction of desire. The crux of the matter is elsewhere: it resides on the seam between pain and pleasure and the mind's reaction to them.

Sensation and thirst

By default, when a person experiences a sensation, a reaction will arise. Such a reaction may be welcoming or resistant, attracted or repelled, coveting or rejecting. Whether powerful or weak, the reaction will come under one of these two categories. Without underestimating the importance of other mental processes and the complex mosaic of contents that makes up our lives as they are, these two categories of reaction – which tend to develop quickly and automatically, as soon as they arise, into craving or "thirst" (*taṇhā*) and then into clinging – play a special role: they occupy a key position in the origination of suffering. According to the second noble truth, the immediate cause of suffering is craving in both its aspects: covetousness and rejection, desire and hate. Desire arises in the face of the pleasant and delightful; hate arises towards the unpleasant and painful. Craving is not merely the direct cause of suffering, it itself is suffering: From the moment it appears, the mind grows tense. Clinging by nature agitates (MN 138).

A craving mind is unable to see reality clearly. This is a mind that, rather than identifying itself and all other things in this world as impermanent and conditioned, and hence by definition bound up with suffering, makes the mistake of perceiving them as permanent and essential entities. We might accept this view of the world, which coheres with what the Buddha taught, and we might see things differently. But even if we do accept this idea intellectually, the deeper strata of our mind remain blind to it. So, when we experience delight we tend to attach ourselves to the experience and fix our grip, ignoring the fact that it is likely to pass soon, leaving us in sorrow or banal discontent – as though that hadn't happened countless times in the past. When we experience pain we tend to react with aversion, tightening our hold on our resentment, forgetting that this pain, too, is mutable, inessential, and not personal. We don't notice how we invest ourselves in efforts to achieve pleasantness and be rid of unpleasantness, while only stimulating the destructive layers of our psyche.

A tortured mind is a confused and clouded mind (Payutto, 1995; VIS 529, 576, 577). And a clouded mind, which doesn't see reality as it is, reacts in a way that generates further suffering. In the Buddhist view, it is the mind's habit to react, out of ignorance, with desire and hate that fuels the infinite, circular, repetitive motion of the process of becoming and of suffering: blindness gives rise to suffering, and suffering gives rise to blindness. It is a vicious cycle in which we are caught up – but not without a way out. The Buddha's teachings propose the following, wonderful paradoxical act: teach this clouded mind to see itself through itself, so as to dissolve the veils of illusion and be released from its prison.

The mind that sees itself

If suffering generates blindness and blindness generates suffering, how can the blind one find a way out of her private hell? The answer lies in the fact that the mind is not one unified essential entity; is a cluster of functions responsible for a number of interdependent processes. The mind's receiving or cognizing part is not the recognizing, labeling, assessing, interpreting part. The feeling part is not the reacting part. (Furthermore, the part that takes in visual input is not the same as that receiving auditory input, or olfactory, or taste-related, or tactile, or intellectual or imaginary.) This is why we can relate differently to each one of these: while nurturing one part, we may dissolve another; sharpening and boosting the first so that it may observe the latter and examine it; developing a wise function that captures inanity, that makes its way through the fog and slowly starts to disperse the habits that cause it.

Among the thirty-one planes of existence, there are some in which those who inhabit them experience sheer delight and others that are tantamount to absolute misery. But for us, humans, a reality that is exclusively pleasure or exclusively pain is not a possibility. Given the fact that the mind has the capacity to examine and analyze itself, what is the advantage of this unavoidable mixture of pleasure and pain? How can this reality, when attended properly, offer a way out of ignorance and suffering? This is the answer, in terms of the Buddha's teaching: Suffering is entailed by reactions of craving and aversion, and these arise by default, as long as the world touches us and triggers sensations. Precisely in this same field, however – and only within this same field – there is a possibility to undo the mind's automatic behavior and its unfortunate consequences. Wherever desire arises, there is an opportunity to eradicate it. Wherever hatred occurs, there is an opportunity to uproot it. But desire arises in the face of pleasantness, and hatred in the presence of unpleasantness; so, in a deeper sense, it is only where pleasure and pain appear that we have the chance to work our way out of craving and aversion, and thus leave behind the world of blindness and misery.

No attempt to become detached from the body and from the pain and pleasure it feels (through self-mortification or certain intense meditative states called *jhāna*) can set the mind free from its defilements, the Buddha understood. Full contact with the entire spectrum of bodily sensations is needed for this purpose (Goenka, 1990). Once one has experienced pleasure and seen it for what it is – impermanent, unsatisfactory, and essenceless – she will not crave and cling to it. If she has experienced pain and seen its true nature, she will not turn away from it or cling to the desire to be rid of it. Experienced and seen: that is, not only by intellectual means but through deep layers of her mind, those that rely on experience and realization. If she succeeds, even for the briefest moment, in not reacting, craving, and clinging,[6] she will begin to free herself from the private prison in which she unknowingly – or at least, without control – revolves.

Even as reaction fuels the continued arising of suffering, so the absence of reaction sets an opposite process into motion. At the first level, these moments of non-reaction enhance the mind's observing part and weaken its reactive part. As the balance of power between the parts of the mind shifts, the ability grows to endure the unpleasant without trying to be rid of it. Here we return to Bion: reduction in the urge to void oneself of components of mental reality, and development of the ability to process them, helps consolidate the connection with reality, that is, with truth.

Building on and flowing from the first level of the process, the second level can be understood when we think of how a fire can be extinguished by depriving it of what it needs in order to burn. If becoming and suffering constitute the fire, then reaction, desire, hate, and clinging are tantamount to the wood and fuel. As long as the mind produces these materials, it adds more fuel to the flames, and they in their turn torture it. Though it is hard to believe that this is what we do to ourselves, it is how we conduct ourselves almost constantly. The practice proposed by the Buddha comes to teach the mind not to react. Each moment the mind manages to do this, it does not allow the fire what it needs to keep burning. When a fire does not get new burning materials, it will start to consume the old. This is the second level of the process: whenever the mind is aware of a sensation and manages to stay balanced – in other words, avoid reacting with either craving or aversion – residues it accumulated when it did react with craving or aversion on earlier, similar occasions start being consumed. It is these residues that cause our suffering: the habits and patterns that make us interpret reality erroneously, to experience it in terms of a misunderstanding, and to react in a manner that makes the fire flare up, which produces suffering both for us and for those around us.

Both levels of the liberation process tie into one another and nourish each other. As the cognizing part and the ability to observe grow stronger at the expense of wrong interpretation and reactivity, more moments occur in which we prevent the flames from getting what they need in order to continue burning. As we don't feed the flames, we force them to devour the old residues. And as the old residues are consumed, the habits that impel us to misinterpret and to react become undone (Barnea-Astrog, 2017).

The objects of desire

At the beginning of life, for a healthy-enough psyche to develop that is able to maintain a reasonable relationship with reality, an accumulation of pleasant experiences associated with contentment and love is required. The mind will be curious and more open to learn from experience depending on how much ability and energy for growth it has (this is not necessarily in a linear relation to how much goodness it was fortunate enough to receive, but it definitely has something to do with that goodness). But even if the mind started its life relatively healthy, it will still need proper nourishment. Like the brain, it goes on absorbing experiences and changing as long as it lives (Doidge, 2008) while it communicates with the environment. If, alongside the inevitable difficulties and challenges, this environment offers plenty of nourishing experiences – attention, support and love, time for being and safe space to develop in – then there is a good chance that the mind (or rather, the body-mind system) will be able to relax and apply curiosity and other resources for learning. If the environment is marked by an almost constant sense of threat and lack, then the body-mind system may be too busy with survival-defensive or compensating activities, and these will reduce it and rob it of a lot of energy. A woman in a relationship without love and warmth; a boy whose classmates constantly harass him; a family struggling to make ends meet, weighed down by debt and worries; a man who tries to somehow manage life while coping with the constraints and incessant pains of intestinal illness – all of them, no matter how different, suffer from chronic conditions linked to the dominant presence of the unpleasant, and this presence affects the way they perceive the world and experience it. They are less likely to be available to deal with developmental tasks that go beyond their demanding everyday burdens. On the other hand, their continuous state of suffering may also push them to seek for further-reaching forms of release than those offered by more common, superficial solutions.

Both what gives pleasure and what causes pain may constrain the psyche or expand it, drench it in a narcissistic or survival-oriented mode of existence, or be the basis for insight. Among other things, this involves the fact that both painful and pleasant experiences can function as foundations for learning but also as objects of desire.

The mind, when not adequately trained (and that means systematic, thorough, and continuous work), reacts to each and every sensation. The type of reaction will depend on the nature of sensation – pleasant, unpleasant, neutral – but every reaction is a reaction, and the mind clings to it and relishes it; and from this clinging and relishing, it derives a kind of pleasure to which it becomes addicted (MN 38).[7] A patient I met with, upon the merest contact with the edges of his abyss of pain, would immediately slip right into it. His breathing would instantaneously accelerate and become labored. His mouth would open a little and his eyes would become glazed, overcast, partly or entirely closing. He would weep, lament, sigh. A terrible pain, a pain that returned just as force-ful, time after time, a pain that refused to be processed. But there was an ecstatic quality to this pain, almost orgasmic (you can quite easily read this short description in terms of pleasure, rather than of pain), and he would more or less lose control. This person was able, to the same extent, to be carried away by sheer delight. Thinking a pleasant thought, full of hope and good omens, he would suddenly notice my eyes, or the song of birds, or the pomelo tree outside, and soar high on the wings of beauty. His gaze would blur, his voice would grow soft, dreamy, and he would be immersed in overflowing pleasantness, forgetful of everything else. Even if the pleasurable object was my eyes, it was not *me* he saw in these moments. He looked in my direction and seemed to be talking to me, but he was not really there with me; he wasn't actually in touch.

And so, both his repeated descents into the depths of sorrow and his fascination with the beautiful and hopeful had a dissociative quality. He would settle on a narrow slice of experience (and the object that triggered it) and detach from the other aspects of the present experience, the current reality, the room, the real-life communication. He would lose perspective and reflective distance, go through whatever he went through, and then eventually return to himself. Carried away by pleasantness or flooded by pain, back and forth, with intervals of full presence and insightful conversation – this is how he was during our meetings. In the course of time, what had been powerful dissociations became more limited discon-nections. He was carried away less often and less intensely, and he grew less helpless when he did. He got better at pulling himself out of these states, back into the room, reason, connection – either unassisted or with my (now less assertive) help. It now happened that he would pull himself away from the edge of the ravine before falling. A mere reminder from me would suffice to make him aware of what was happening (a process whose unfolding he had learned to foresee) and shake him up out of his trance.

What we went through is interesting and important for several other reasons. Here I describe it because it shows simply that pain, too, can be an object of desire; that suffering, too, can act like an object of addic-tion. "Pain is hatred's way of taking pleasure in death, just like delight and love are the way we take pleasure in life" (Durban, 2003; Segal, 1993). The mind is addicted to its own behavior: its reactions and thirst are what fuel its ongoing, repetitive becoming, which involves the ongo-ing appearance of reactions and thirst. And thus, the mental motion of craving relates to both desire and hatred: the life instincts and the death instincts, the thirst for existence and the thirst for annihilation – all are fundamentally thirst. From this perspective, the essential dichotomy between pain and pleasure withers, and what we remain with is the mental action one directs at them – this is what determines their function: addictive objects, fuel for the process of suffering – or alternatively, objects of investigation, tools to uproot reactive habits.

Let us now return to the pleasurable sensations, which, too, may serve, as said, to support or delay liberation, as foundation for growth or as objects of desire. Where they are a foundation for growth, on the one hand they offer a strong, flexible, and open mental-physical basis, and on the other they give the investigating mind the opportunity to recognize their impermanent, unsatisfactory, and inessential nature, and thus to set itself free of craving for them. As objects of desire, they fan craving and hence suffering and delusion; they intensify reactivity and clinging and interfere with one's ability to discern. I have already touched on some aspects of this, focusing especially on necessary goodness. Now I would like to elaborate on the difference between the two functions of the pleasurable, and how the mind moves between them.

A simple illustration of pleasurable sensations that function as objects of desire is alcohol and drugs. People use intoxicants because they arouse pleasurable sensations and soothe unpleasurable ones. A shy and insecure man may feel more confident after three glasses of wine. An anxious and preoccupied woman, after three glasses of wine, may feel relaxed and calm. He does not like his shyness; he is uptight, uneasy in his chair. She suffers from her anxiety which turns her into a nervous wreck, never at peace. They drink and the unpleasantness vanishes. They drink and a nice feeling spreads through their body, accompanied by good mood. It is only natural that they wish to expel the oppressive feelings attending insecurity and anxiety and to invoke the pleasant feelings of confidence and tranquility. But somewhere deep down in the mind, behind the scenes, those pleasurable feelings they yearn for so badly only fan their intolerance of unpleasure and their craving of pleasure, and in this way they amplify their suffering.

Religions and various spiritual traditions include the use of intoxicants in their customs, and secular culture, too, without too much difficulty has adopted the use of some of them. One can refer to spiritual experiences that people have as a result of taking intoxicants, in certain conditions: visions and revelations and feelings of at-oneness with the universe and sublime joy. But if we remember the different parts of the mind, we realize that the outcome of using these intoxicants is the exact opposite of what Buddhist meditation aims for. Buddhist practice is designed to develop the part that takes in reality-as-it-is and to weaken the part that interprets it falsely according to past residues that have accumulated in the mind. It seeks to develop the part that wisely observes and to weaken (or entirely dissolve, in the end) the reactive part. Drugs and alcohol usually weaken the part that takes in reality-as-it-is and embolden the part that interprets erroneously, while adding new residues that will serve as material for future reference. They damage the part that observes wisely and at the same time stir up the mind, making it crave, thereby fanning its reactive part. This is one of the main reasons why avoidance of intoxicants is part of the way to liberation, as the Buddha taught it.

Subtle pleasantness

The case of intoxicants is a relatively clear-cut illustration. The mind can in fact respond in a similar manner to anything that entails a desirable sensation, whether it is a sight, a sound, taste, smell, touch, memory, image, emotion or thought. If this is so, then it can make similar use of the pleasant feelings that are the result of meditative states. In the practice of Vipassana or Satipaṭṭhāna (*Satipaṭṭhāna*) – the systematic observation of the body and its sensations and the mind and its contents – the meditator methodically analyzes his mind-body system; the illusion of the solidity and permanence of this same system is the source of suffering. When he focuses on his bodily sensations as a meeting point between the physical and the mental and between conscious and unconscious, he experiences the gradual dissolving of the sense of physical solidity, and along with it the sense of the solid self. In this process of undoing, various residual elements arise from the depths of the mind. Once there, if they are recognized as impermanent and don't trigger reactions of either craving or aversion, there is an opportunity to dissolve them. This dissolving comes with a delicate stream of very pleasant sensations which temporarily replace the sensations of pain, discomfort, or dullness that were previously present in different areas of the body. These pleasant sensations also relate to the fact that the more one progresses in analyzing the causes of suffering, mental factors develop that support happiness, calmness, and liberation. Some of these factors are accompanied by very pleasant states of mind (and bodily sensations); while they can be precious sources of support on the way, they may also constitute a danger to those who experience them.

One group of positive elements that develops as part of this process is called "the seven factors of enlightenment". The first three of these are awareness (or mindfulness), investigation of truth, and effort (or energy investment). As these develop, three further factors arise in the meditator, which are associated with subtle pleasant sensations. First a physical and mental state of rapture or supreme joy arises and grows, which, though very subtle, may also be intense. Waves of this pleasure rise and wane, one after the other, to eventually result in the next component: deep tranquility. This condition is marked by such quiet and calmness that only an extremely sharp and wakeful mind will register the tiny changes that nevertheless occur below the surface. Deep tranquility supports the emergence of the next factor of enlightenment – concentration (Goenka, 2010).[8] In this state, the mind is sharp, collected, and all immersed in its object of observation. Undisturbed immersion is without question one of the most profound pleasures a person can experience. The seventh factor of enlightenment is mental equilibrium, the non-reactive quality whose cultivation, like that of awareness, accompanies each step in the process (Goenka, 2010).

As the mind gets addicted to sensations and desire rather than the object itself, any object whatsoever can become addictive. Since any object can become a source of addiction, the Buddha warned against the dangers of the particularly pleasant experiences I described. When one experiences rapture, the mind risks developing craving and attachment because it is so pleasurable. When one feels deep tranquility, the risk is that the mind will fail to perceive the transient nature of the very delicate sensations at its basis, attach itself to the profound stillness in it, and mistake it for an objective rather than the temporary rest it actually is (Goenka, 2010).

Being drawn by states of meditative immersion and fixating on them is simply another manifestation of the same basic tendency towards clinging and pleasure, and it should be recognized as a danger (MN 138). The use of the word *danger* or *risk*, however, should not suggest that these states are to be avoided. If they are properly approached by the one who experiences them, they are most valuable. Pleasant experiences that are the result of right meditative practice do have significant liberative qualities, since they weaken attachment to sensual desire (Arbel, 2015), and for other reasons as well. The joy of concentration or immersion, for example, offers a subtle alternative to sensual pleasures and reduces the need for the emotional gratification they offer. It provides a place of rest and rehabilitation when the mind becomes blunted or when it needs encouragement before being ready to divest itself of some more illusions, recognize its faults, and abandon its cravings. The equilibrium and sharpness of concentration help cultivate a strong sensitivity which enables one to take note of the most subtle degrees of discontent. They provide the mind with the necessary balance to stay focused in the moment, to penetrate superficial reality and reach insight (Thanissaro Bhikkhu, 1996). In addition, in the same way exactly that the anger, anxiety, and impatience a person experiences might reduce and harden him, and just as they trickle through to his surroundings and affect it, the joy, pleasure, sobriety, and serenity of the factors of enlightenment will naturally expand him and will naturally spread and distribute themselves, especially where they are charged with non-egocentric feelings of love and compassion. It is for all these reasons that the enhancement of the factors of enlightenment is an integral part of the path that leads to the gentle and subtle.

Subtle pleasure forms the basis for tranquility; tranquility forms the basis for concentration; all of them together sustain equanimity and clear vision. But this is on condition that they are devoid of desire. Desire blurs and agitates. If the (mature) mind, in other words, knows how to employ rapture, tranquility, and concentrated immersion in the same way it uses (both in its early days and in maturity) "necessary goodness" – as a supportive resource that gives it the strength to cope with pain, to be in touch with reality, and to love – then these factors function as a means of liberation. If the mind treats them as objects of desire, then it obstructs its own way, further entangling itself in misery-generating patterns for the sake of a moment's pleasure.

And so, while pleasant sensations can fortify the mind, from Buddhism's perspective, even the most subtle pleasure is not the objective. The objective is to traverse the entire field of sensations in awareness of its nature: transient, conditioned, bound up with suffering, impersonal, lacking selfhood. Since every mental event is attended by sensation, when one crosses the field of sensations, she is actually crossing the whole of the psycho-physical sphere. A thorough investigation of the psycho-physical field, one that ignores nothing – or, in western psychological terms, that leaves no mental process unconscious – of necessity leads to what is beyond this field: the immutable, the unconditioned, what is not bound up with suffering, which is also impersonal and lacking selfhood: *nibbāna* (Sanskrit: *nirvāṇa*).

One who fully investigates her sensations and understands their nature will have purified her mind from all elements of suffering (SN 36.12). One who experienced sensations as they are, who witnessed their appearance and disappearance, the pleasure they hold, the danger, and the way to be released from them – this person becomes independent, liberated as a result of non-clinging (DN 1).

***

Suffering is associated with blindness and thirst, emerges from them and leads into them. Blindness and thirst are related to solidity and hardness. The path dissolves, refines, and clarifies: what was solid dissolves, what was hard softens, and pleasantness replaces pain, at times, or is revealed as an undercurrent that flows along with it. Goodness is necessary in order to build some of the most important resources of the mind at the outset of life, and to continue nourishing it throughout its course; this goodness is associated with pleasant sensations. Pleasantness is necessary, but as soon as the mind begins to covet it, it changes status, becoming the object of instinctual gratification. Wallowing in pain causes suffering, adding oil to the flames, but recognizing pain as a characteristic of existence can set into motion an opposite process in which all the factors of liberation and enlightenment emerge (SN 12.23). Both the pleasant and the unpleasant are necessary: identifying them as non-personal and bound up with suffering is inseparably part of complete knowledge. The sober experience of pleasure and pain is what allows us to undo the roots of suffering: ignorance, desire, and hate.

Notes

1 For this reason, they are also unable to hear the Buddha's teaching or otherwise come into contact with it.
2 Of course, some beings in higher realms are endowed with virtues and wisdom that support them in seeking release from *saṃsāra* while they dwell in their present fortunate state.
3 The infant seems to come into the world with a preconception of the breast, and with some expectation of the breast materializing and filling the sense of void that attends hunger. When the breast fails to materialize, hunger arises, followed by fear of death. The encounter between preconception and non-materialization produces "pre-thought". The latter may be immediately evacuated through projective identification or undergo transformation and become thought (Gampel, 2004).
4 Through projective identification.
5 Actually saw them, as he travelled out of the palace (like the previous Buddha, Vipassī), or only contemplating old age, sickness, and death – regarding this, there are different versions in early texts.
6 I refer to the following three links: *saṅkhāra, taṇhā*, and *upādāna*, the fuel that feeds further through the process of arising and passing – saṃsāra.
7 Originally: "So evaṃ anurodhavirodhaṃ samāpanno yaṃ kiñci vedanaṃ vedeti sukhaṃ vā dukkhaṃ vā adukkhamasukhaṃ vā, so taṃ vedanaṃ abhinandati abhivadati ajjhosāya tiṭṭhati. Tassa taṃ vedanaṃ abhinandato abhivadato ajjhosāya tiṭṭhato uppajjati nandī. Yā vedanāsu nandī tadupādānaṃ, tassupādānapaccayā bhavo, bhavapaccayā jāti, jātipaccayā jarāmaraṇaṃ sok aparidevadukkhadomanassupāyāsā sambhavanti. Evametassa kevalassa dukkhakkhandhassa samudayo hoti."

Engaged in satisfaction and resistance, he relishes any sensation he feels –
pleasure, pain, neither-pleasure-nor-pain – welcomes it, and remains fastened
to it. As he relishes that sensation, welcomes it, and remains fastened to it,
delight arises. [But] delighting in sensations is clinging. From clinging as a
condition, [the process of] becoming arises. From [the process of] becoming
as a condition, birth arises. From birth as a condition, aging and death arise,
along with sorrow, lamentation, physical and mental pain, and tribulations.
Thus arises this entire mass of suffering. (MN 38: 404)
    In translating this, I was also helped by Thanissaro Bhikkhu's translation
(2011).
8 The original Pāli names of these factors of enlightenment are *sati*, *dhamma-
vicaya*, *vīriya*, *pīti*, *passaddhi*, *samādhi*, and *upekkhā*. The factor of awareness
(*sati*), here, is synonymous with the seventh aspect of the eightfold path –
"right awareness" or "right mindfulness" (*sammā-sati*). The meditator's ability to be aware develops from the start and accompanies all the other factors
that arise or dissolve in her. When some liberation-supporting factor develops
in her or doesn't, she is aware of it. When a harmful factor dissolves in her or
doesn't, she is aware of it. The investigation of the truth or of the law of nature
(*dhamma-vicaya*) is an analytic-dismantling quality that the mind develops:
on the intellectual level, but first and foremost on the level of direct experience. Effort, or energy investment (*vīriya*), is a quality synonymous with
"right effort" (*sammā-vāyāmo*), which is the sixth aspect on the eightfold path.
This is a balanced effort to develop the beneficial or wholesome and to undo
the destructive or unwholesome, which is wholly invested in mere observation
and does not cling to outcomes. *Pīti* is a difficult word to translate and can be
rendered as "bliss", "delight", "thrill", or "joy" – each of which captures an
aspect of this experience (Goenka, 1998). The factor of *samādhi* can take a
variety of shapes, but in Buddhist teaching it is synonymous with the seventh
aspect on the path – *sammā-samādhi*, right concentration. Right concentration
allies itself with the other components of the path, which are associated with
moral behavior and a realistic view of reality. The objects of right concentration are therefore those which are not based on ignorance, desire, or hate.

References

Alvarez, A. (2012). *The Thinking Heart: Three Levels of Psychoanalytic Ther-
apy with Disturbed Children*. Hove: Routledge.
AN 10.58.
Arbel, K. (2015). The liberative role of jhānic joy (pīti) and pleasure (sukha) in the
early Buddhist path to awakening. *Buddhist Studies Review*, *32* (2): 179–205.
Balint, M. (1968). *The Basic Fault: Therapeutic Aspects of Regression*. New
York: Brunner/Mazel.
Barnea-Astrog, M. (2015). Internal holding, external holding: three experiences
in primitive fear of annihilation. *Hebrew Psychology*. Accessed May 18, 2015
at: www.hebpsy.net/articles.asp?id=3252.
Barnea-Astrog, M. (2017). *Carved by Experience: Vipassana, Psychoanalysis,
and the Mind Investigating Itself*. London: Karnac.

Bion, W. R. (1959). Attacks on linking. *International Journal of PsychoAnalysis*, *40*: 308–315.

Bion, W. R. (1962a). The psycho-analytic study of thinking. *International Journal of Psycho-Analysis*, *43*: 306–310.

Bion, W. R. (1962b). *Learning from Experience*. London: Tavistock. DN 1.

Doidge, N. (2008). *The Brain That Changes Itself*. London: Penguin.

Durban, J. (2003). On love, hatred and anxiety – an introduction to Kleinian thinking. In: J. Durban (Ed.), *Melanie Klein: Selected Writings* (pp. 7–38). Tel Aviv: Bookwarm.

Durban, J. & Roth, M. (2013). Introduction to: *Melanie Klein: Selected Writings Vol. 2*. (pp. 11–40). Tel Aviv: Bookworm.

Epstein, M. (2015). On the seashore of endless worlds: Buddha and Winnicott. In: A. Hoffer (Ed.), *Freud and the Buddha: The Couch and the Cushion* (pp. 89–108). London: Karnac.

Freud, S. (1911). Formulations on the two principles of mental functioning. *S.E.*, *12*: 213–226.

Freud, S. (1920). Beyond the pleasure principle. *S.E.*, *18:* 1–64.

Gampel, Y. (2004). Introduction to: Wilfred R. Bion, *Learning from Experience*. Tel Aviv: Bookworm.

Goenka, S. N. (1990). *The Importance of Vedanā and Sampajañña*. Igatpuri: Vipassana Research Institute.

Goenka, S. N. (1998). *Mahāsatipaṭṭhāna Sutta: The Great Discourse on the Establishing of Awareness*. Igatpuri: Vipassana Research Institute.

Goenka, S. N. (2010). *Discourses on Satipaṭṭhāna Sutta*. Igatpuri: Vipassana Research Institute.

Grotstein, J. S. (1995). Projective identification reappraised – projective identification, introjective identification, the transference/countertransference neurosis/psychosis, and their consummate expression in the crucifixion, the Pietà, and "Therapeutic Exorcism," Part II: The countertransference complex. *Contemporary Psychoanalysis*, *31*: 479–520.

Klein, M. (1946). Notes on some schizoid mechanisms. *International Journal of Psychoanalysis*, *27*: 99–110.

Klein, M. (1975a). Some theoretical conclusions regarding the emotional life of the infant. In: M. M. R. Khan (Ed.), *Envy and Gratitude and Other Works 1946–1963* (pp. 61–93). London: Hogarth & the Institute of Psycho-Analysis.

Klein, M. (1975b). Envy and gratitude. In: M. M. R. Khan (Ed.), *Envy and Gratitude and Other Works 1946–1963* (pp. 176–235). London: Hogarth & the Institute of Psycho-Analysis.

Kurtz, R., Martin, D. & Sparks, F. (2013). The practice of loving presence for therapists. *Ron Kurtz Hakomi Educational Materials*. Accessed September 2, 2013 at: hakomi.com/ron-kurtz-educational-materials/refined-hakomi-books/the-practice-of-loving-presence-book-3.

Lazar, R., & Erlich, H. S. (1996). Repetition compulsion. *Psychoanalysis and Contemporary Thought*, *19*: 29–55.

MN 38.

MN 138.

Ogden, T. H. (2004). *The Primitive Edge of Experience*. Lanham, MD: Rowman & Littlefield.

Payutto, P. A. (1995). *Dependent Origination: The Buddhist Law of Conditionality*. Translated by Bruce Evans. Thailand: Buddhadhamma Foundation.

Pelled, E. (2005). *Psychoanalysis and Buddhism: On the Human Capacity to Know*. Tel Aviv: Resling.

Segal, H. (1993). On the clinical usefulness of the concept of the death instinct. *International Journal of Psycho-Analysis*, *74*: 55–61.

SN 12.23.

SN 35.135.

SN 36.12.

SN 56.48.

Symington, J. & Symington, N. (1996). *The clinical thinking of Wilfred Bion*. Hove: Routledge.

Thanissaro Bhikkhu (1996). Wings to awakening: part III. *Access to Insight*. Accessed October 3, 2016 at: www.accesstoinsight.org/lib/authors/thanissaro/wings/part3.html.

Thanissaro Bhikkhu (2011). A translation of Mahatanhasankhaya Sutta: The Greater Craving-Destruction Discourse (MN 38). *Access to Insight*. Accessed November 27, 2017 at: www.accesstoinsight.org/tipitaka/mn/mn.038.than.html.

VIS 529.

VIS 576.

VIS 577.

Winnicott, D. W. (1974). Fear of breakdown. *International Review of Psycho-Analysis*, *1*: 103–107.

Winnicott, D. W. (1975). Primary maternal preoccupation. In: *Through Paediatrics to Psycho-Analysis* (pp. 300–305). London: Hogarth & the Institute of Psycho-Analysis.

Winnicott, D. W. (1987). *Babies and Their Mothers*. Cambridge: Perseus.

Winnicott, D. W. (2016). Ego distortion in terms of true and false Self. In: L. Caldwell & H. Taylor Robinson (Ed.). *The Collected Works of D. W. Winnicott: Volume 6, 1960–1963* (pp. 159–174). New York: Oxford University.

Chapter 4

A home in the universe

The substances of our sensitivity are the pleasant and the unpleasant, as well as the objects of the senses – the elements in the world – which evoke pleasantness or unpleasantness as they touch us. All of us are sensitive to contact with the world; gentle people perhaps even more so. Equipped with a thin empathic wall (Nathanson, 1986), a not quite sealed or not quite dead insulating layer (if such a layer exists), the surrounding world penetrates them at a high resolution. Its qualities, whether nourishing or hurtful, leave considerable traces. Being so exposed, how can they find themselves a home and feel protected?

A feeling of being at home occurs when the senses, the nervous system, or mental and physical activity attain a certain degree of comfort, a state of reasonable calmness in which they are not required constantly to fight off impressions impinging from outside and to manage their inner reactions to these. In this state the system is open to experience and to learning from it. A sense of being at home depends on inner as well as outer conditions, each supporting the other. Thus, the more a person learns about herself in a non-condemning mental space, the more clarity she gains about her mutually arising relations with the world, and this enables her – circumstances allowing – to steer herself to a compatible and positive human and non-human environment. Nina's case bears this out. The longer a person dwells in a compatible and positive environment, the more perceptive, attentive, and non-condemning feedback she receives; this will help her inner lucidity evolve and support ease and nourishment to rise and take root in her. Louise found a home in this intra-psychic and interpersonal zone, one in which curious and loving attention examined processes of discord and attunement, restored a clarity that had been distorted, and enabled an increasing degree of comfort and nourishment.

We may think of a process like the one Louise went through in Winnicottian terms such as holding function, true and false self, core and shell. The mother – or the care-giving, attentive figure, the one who accompanies, who adapts herself or himself – holds all potential healthy developments of the one being held (Matri, 2005). If she does this well enough, then an authentic self will emerge in the baby, the child, Louise, enabling them to attain a sufficient body-mind harmony. Should she fail, then the child may either lose faith in her body or have to invest her mental energy in her environment, trying to make sure it is well and strong enough to continue caring for her. In this case "the center of gravity of [her] being"[1] will not be able to "afford to lodge [. . .] in the kernel" (Winnicott, 1975, p. 99) and to grow from within it. She will have to channel a lot of her resources to the maintenance of her external envelope – the shell. In other words, she will have no choice but to constitute her own envelope (Matri, 2005). If this person, later in life, has access to good conditions – for instance, as part of a therapeutic relationship – then at least part of the distortion may be undone; then at least some of the resources may let go of dealing with the envelope, and at least some improvement in the harmony of body and mind can be attained. (Of course, we should remember that a person's own characteristics play a crucial role: it is not only the mothering-environment, the therapeutic-environment, or the environment in general that make a difference.)

The home or shelter that a person's gentleness makes for itself in the world is, in this sense, the holding envelope and adjusted attention. If gentleness is not mere sensitivity but also involves an ethical position regarding sensitivity, then this home should offer ethical shelter, a sort of shelter that is related to truth. Winnicott, in this context, suggests a certain layer of truth: The home protects the tender core, from which a true, not false, personality may arise. The home protects the core from a catastrophic state of un-becoming, disintegration, from the terror of collapse; and it protects it from the falsehood produced by the mechanisms appointed to address the catastrophe when these are forced, in the absence of adequate protection, to become rigid.

The distinction between a true and false self harks back to the modern (as well as ancient) assumption that people have a clear and unambiguous core. Those who point out the problematic potential of this distinction, it may be said, represent the postmodern approach, which doubts the existence of such a well-defined self (Berman, 2009).[2]

Winnicott himself, actually, never intended such an exaggerated dichotomy between true and false self or to encourage a demonization of the false self (ibid.). He situated them on a continuum consisting of five levels reflecting different interrelations between true and false self, and he also stressed the positive, protective role of the false self (Winnicott, 2016). So, neither the author of the notion, nor his critics, concede to simplistic interpretations: they look for a more complex understanding of the lively and authentic and of the less lively and less authentic (Berman, 2009). Still, the point of doing so seems to be that we don't ignore or exclude any part of the self, rather than to see better beyond the self in general.

Adjusted attention, in principle, implies an ethical position of non-violence towards the experiencing subject and towards experience as such; a position that safeguards, according to Winnicott, the truth of the personality. However, since gentleness and the ethics we are interested in refer to a truth that penetrates the nucleus of the self, touching on universal processes of becoming, suffering, and release from suffering – like those the Buddha's teachings describe – we cannot settle for notions like "the true self", no matter how rich and profound they are. The formulation I suggested above, that when a person is at home she is open to learning from experience, may help us ahead at this point. If we follow Bion's thinking, there are, among the conditions and states of mind that support learning from experience, some that don't intuitively connect with a sense of being at home. These include non-familiarity, non-holding on to the known, faith in the unknowable, and lingering in frustrating, formless, daunting states. The path Bion opens up to us aims for contact with a dimension of truth that is located beyond the desiring self, and this is the reason why I choose to take it. However, let's add a layer to it. If we understand that the ability to make contact with the truth is in inverse relation to the presence of memory, desire, expectation, and the need to comprehend (according to Bion), and in inverse relation to the presence of the roots of suffering – ignorance, desire, and hate (according to the Buddha) – we must go on and ask: How can the gentle person find the kind of shelter that does not allow these factors to take over her mental life and suffocate it, but instead creates a climate that enables her to see through them and be released? Since both taking over and release occur at the deepest substrate of the mind, our discussion has to delve into the darkness and chaos of becoming and fear which reign there, then to feel our way out using the light cast by the concepts of "knowledge" and "faith".

Becoming, separation, and fear

> Only suffering arises when anything arises. Only suffering ceases
> when anything ceases.
>
> –(SN 12.15)

The Pāli word for "world" or "universe" is *loka*, and it is the entire phe-
nomenal world: the world of mind and of matter, the inner world and the
outer world. When we look inside ourselves and investigate our inner
reality through Vipassana, we conduct a simultaneous, two-fold analysis
of phenomena. As we break them up into constituent elements and particles on the one hand, we are also aware, on the other, of the links between
them. Investigation of the inner world shows us laws, laws within laws,
minute laws, and ostensible paradoxes, which on closer inspection stand
revealed as expressions of different layers of reality. These layers of reality, together with the laws that structure them, coexist and interweave,
approach and detach, creating the tissue – alive and kicking, constantly
changing – of the flow of life. The world we perceive as internal is
reflected in the world we perceive as external, and vice versa: the same
laws, layers of reality, and interrelations express themselves through
mind and body, through the meditator's and the psychologist's objects
of investigation, or through those of the physicist, the astronomer, and
the biologist. Fleischman (2013) described how the tide of scientific discoveries of recent decennia has resulted in a cultural and psychological
revolution, a fundamental change in the way we see, feel, and experience
ourselves and the universe. Discoveries in physics, chemistry, biology,
and astronomy teach us about the macro and the micro, the galaxy and
the cell. They instruct us about the matter and energy from which we are
made, the matter and energy that constitute the universe, about the channels of information, the interconnections, the rules and uncertainty that
underlie the incessant processes of creation and decay inside as well as
around us. They teach us about ourselves and about the world, about ourselves in the world, about ourselves as a manifestation of the world. This
irruption of knowledge and its seepage into our way of thinking amount
to a breakup of the old world order: "We are inheritors of moments when
the constrictions of ignorance and belief were eliminated by contrary
evidence, moments when our psychological worldview opened into
more unrestricted and inconclusive questions and exploration" (Fleischman, 2013, p. 320). It is true that large parts of humanity live in soci-
eties dominated by rigid beliefs and dogmatic structures, but they too

are affected by this essential change. Their beliefs and dogmas have to survive tsunamis of contradictory, clashing information. In the face of these profound changes and the shattering and disappearance of familiar views – which, by way of one alternative, may be held on to with extra force in a refractory reality – what remains of the sense of being at home and safe, of stability and solidity? What is the status of stability and solidity in such a reality, and isn't the notion of living with a sense of security chimerical – or can there be a security grounded in clear vision? How does this huge cultural-psychological shift associate itself with the fear of breakdown and annihilation described by psychoanalysis? And how does it amplify this fear, reflect it, or cast light on it? Since the different levels of reality – micro and macro, personal and universal, internal and external, mental and material – are mutually inflected, affecting and illuminating one another, I will move between them in discussing the domain of investigation outlined by the above questions.

The big bang

Bion described psychic reality and thinking as originating, in part, in a type of "catastrophic emotional explosion" (1970, p. 14) or "Big Bang" (Eigen, 1985, p. 323). As long as the particles resulting from this explosion and strewn around every which way stay in their raw state – separate in one sense, yet welded together in another – catastrophe maintains its total, original form, all-pervasive, meaningless and unprocessed, spreading "through the infantile cosmos with infinite horror, a kind of electrocution from no tangible source" (Eigen, 1985, p. 324). Even when they are processed, the rudimentary particles preserve the traces of their catastrophic sources (Eigen, 1985).

I opened this book with Ron's sense of terror, the insufferable pain filling his entire being, the unknowable chasm at the very bottom of existence, an existence naturally painful and inextricably bound up with separation: "Everything I passed was something that was about to pass away. Every moment a moment of parting. In the mere passage of time there loomed separation. Separation filled each and every moment, insufferable pain". It was only during travel, when an external force bore him along, that terror was prevented from arising. This was probably the result of the sense of continuity, the sense of no-hiatus, which smoothens gaps in time and space. A sense of there being a whole (a whole self, a whole world, perhaps), rather than fragmentation, worked to soften the pain of separation, the pain of the ephemeral, of the chasm, of distance. Eigen (1985) asked: Is the element of distance inherent in the sense of catastrophe? Does it reside in the sense of catastrophe a priori? Is catastrophe experienced as catastrophe exactly because it is characterized by the element of distance?

The mind works in order to suppress distance and erase it, to blur and deny it. It tries hard to bridge the gaps, close the spaces, to tighten, to continue and not stop. But these actions actually confirm the very existence of distance, dissemination, and separation, and testify to their insufferable, catastrophic nature. Of course, the mind also works hard to separate, like in the case of classic Freudian projection, and to disperse, like in the case of attacks on linking and projection of minute fragments of the personality that Bion described (1957, 1959). Still, at some very primal level, consciousness plays a cohesive, continuity-generating function, as I will soon explain. Either way, distance is a product of explosion, and in this sense, a sign of catastrophe; but in the absence of a primary distance, nothing can emerge. This explains why, from Bion's perspective, there is no self without a sense of catastrophe, and without a sense of catastrophe there is no self:

> The sense of catastrophe *links* aspects of personality [even for those whose self and sense of catastrophe failed to properly appear, or appeared but then seemed to have disappeared (Bion, 1970; Eigen, 1985)]. It is the cement that holds personality together, a primordial forming principle, the sea or atmosphere we live in. In psychosis personality itself is an ongoing catastrophe. But Bion's vision goes beyond the conventionally pathological. The sense of catastrophe already seems to have had a history when the infant first screams and perhaps is older than life itself.
>
> (Eigen, 1985, p. 325)

The cement, the connecting tissue, is the result of fragmentation. Into this general element certain contents are poured: the terror of death, for instance, or the terror of birth or of change, the fear of what devours, of sickness, castration, fire, falling, drowning, suffocation, leakage and the lack of boundaries (Eigen, 1985). All these and others are specific instances of the catastrophic element that, like a fundamental characteristic, runs through experience, pointing at a larger truth: coming into being involves an explosion, a disintegration, the parting and diffusion of particles away from each other. It involves the catastrophe of separation. "Emotional life bears the imprint of the combustible/conservative universe in which it grows. Given the nature of the universe we are part of, it seems inevitable that cataclysm is a formative pole of our beings" (Eigen, 1985, p. 325). If, then, we direct our attention away from the internal universe to the external, we are bound to discover similar spectacles.

The notion of a big bang and the discovery that the universe is constantly expanding or dispersing situate us in a living and dynamic universe, a moving and changing universe whose beginning and end themselves are a function of change. The universe, however, does not simply expand. Two competing teams of physicists who received the 2012 Nobel Prize in Physics found that this expansion is accelerated. This finding clashes with the earlier view that gravitation will eventually cause this movement of expansion to come to an end (Fleischman, 2013). Isn't this alarming? The initial catastrophe, the process of parting set into motion by the big bang, neither comes to a halt nor is expected to do so. Its speed actually increases. Separation, disintegration, distance, dissemination . . . an endless expansion, which, when it is the object of thought and touches a certain mind at a certain moment in time, may cause it to expand similarly, and when it touches another mind, or the same one at a different moment, may horrify.

The universe is not only defined by means of this explosion but the resulting motion also accelerates (Fleischman, 2013). Constant instability and change do not only characterize the sphere of our existence: they themselves lack stability and change constantly: "The rate of change is changing. The origin was change and the expansion keeps changing" (Fleischman, 2013, p. 325). We sense a similar acceleration in the rate of change in our everyday life. Scientific and informational revolutions affect our daily lives at an increasingly rapid, dizzying pace. (In fact, this is how things are even if we don't refer to the context and the historical juncture. Impermanence and mutability are fundamental features of a reality in which the infinity of factors making up each and every material and mental moment fuel the infinity of factors of the next. The visible pace of change, however, its quality and the characteristics of the shifting phenomena, are singularly defined in relation to each phenomenon, place, and era.) Such a reality reveals that there is no solid and permanent anchor, essential and enduring. "The eternal heavens aren't. We are the first generations to live in a dynamic universe. Humankind has always imagined that stars are eternal, symbolic of the enduring transcendent – but not anymore, not to us" (Fleischman, 2013, p. 333). Solidity and permanence only exist as an illusion, and illusion, too, naturally, possesses neither solidity nor permanence. Not even the notion of the big bang offers a clear-cut answer to existential waverings, nor does it point at an absolute beginning or end. Even if this explosion (and there might never have been such a singular event but rather an ongoing series of smaller explosions) marks the emergence of our particular present world, it clearly does not signal the beginnings of time and space (Fleischman, 2013). So, in terms of our ability to hold tight to an orderly, reassuring notion of the world, we are on shaky ground: "Psychologically speaking, we inhabit a new world that has no envelope, no dominant narrative, no container" (Fleischman, 2013, p. 321).

> The stars are now in space, not in heaven, and our planets are like sparks from a campfire. We fly through space on a cinder. The moon is not a goddess but is part of us, some lost material, our own leftovers. The solar system is new and doomed. Our universe is ruled by change. The stars are not in a heaven exempt from change and death. Nor are they exempt from our study and insight. We live in a psychological worldview in which no thing, no material, is fixed, steady, free of the master wand of entropy, change, dispersal. [. . .] We are the first large group of beings for whom transience is the central fact. When we look up into the night sky, we see our own origin, our end, our vulnerability, our motility, our incomprehensibility.
>
> (Fleischman, 2013, p. 334)

The mind seeks something to hold onto in this ever-accelerating universe, a universe that started in an explosion. And it goes on doing so in a reality in which prevailing dogmas, beliefs and ideas (engendered by other human beings who themselves emerged from this universe) shatter at an increasing rate. From its fragmented universe the mind looks for something to follow. Like the infant who fixes his attention on a monotonous sound or on the light of the lamp in order not to experience the catastrophe of being dropped brought about by the loss of his mother's attention, the mind pursues sense objects to which it might cling. Like the infant who keeps moving so as to have a sense of going-on-being, it tries not to stop and look inside, tries constantly to be in motion. Like the infant who contracts his muscles to feel tight rather than diffuse, the mind contracts itself around the dogmas, ideas and beliefs which the flow of information has already punctured and shattered and made superfluous in almost every possible way.

The Buddha said: "There is such a time as when this world system gets dissolved, as it does at times, after a lapse of many aeons. [. . .] there is such a time as when this world system arises again, as it does at times, after a lapse of many aeons" (DN 27, in: U Ko Lay, 2005, pp. 98–99). From his broad perspective, stretching across time spans of unimaginable proportions, he could see that the world expands and contracts alternatingly, evolves and dissolves. In the Pāli language, the word for "dissolves" (or "contracts") and the word for "evolves" (or "develops" or "expands") refer, on the one hand, to opposite motions: dissolving as opposed to evolving, contraction as opposed to expansion; in certain contexts, one is sometimes translated as "destruction" and the other as "renewal".[3] In another sense, though, both denote renewal or a new beginning, and both suggest the fundamental process of change (Rhys Davids & Stede, 1921–1925, p. 637). We disintegrate because we come into being. We decay because we become. Creation and annihilation plug into each other, and this is why nothing continues into eternity or is a priori perfect in itself. The terror of nullification, of leakage and dissolution, of disintegration and un-integration, is a part of us and accompanies us simply because we are, in our very essence, perishable phenomena in a perishable universe: non-solid phenomena that disperse into space, falling apart from moment to moment, separating from ourselves. And so the answer to Eigen's question seems to be positive: Distance is inherent to the sense of catastrophe because it is inherent to the process of creation and decay, and awareness of this (even if the mental layers in which this awareness inheres are considered "unconscious" in psychoanalytic terms) produces feelings of devastation and dread.

Devastation is related to separation. Separation is distance, in time and in space. Distance is inherent to the process of evolving and dissolving: of man and world. The distance between one moment and the next, between the particles of the atom, between the particles of the mind; distance, which approaches the infinite or zero, distance which is all-embracing even as it is minute.

In the very cradle of our being lie together fragmentation and rupture, unification and continuity, all entangled. The sense of continuity depends on fragmentation, and fragmentation depends on the sense of continuity (Eigen, 1985). We move along the line that stretches between (concealed) dissolution and (visible) solidification, pulling ourselves together – whether ingeniously or in terror – from the abyss between becoming and decay.

A big bang – an end that is a beginning – involves the dispersal of the particles produced by explosion. The catastrophe of dispersal is inherent to the feeling of "I". The suffering of annihilation is a fundamental characteristic of existence.

Truth and faith: following the signs of existence

If the suffering entailed by becoming and decaying is inherent to existence, then those who wish to be aware of reality-as-it-is must become cognizant of it. The three marks of existence, according to the Buddha, are change, suffering, and the absence of selfhood; once we are clearly aware of one of these, we will inevitably become, at some point, aware of the others. If terror is the mind's tormenting response to processes of becoming and decaying, to impermanence, disintegration, and fragmentation, then they are what it points at. To know the latter, therefore, we can make use of the former: we may look in the direction to which this terror points.

Some words about memory, desire, and knowledge

According to Bion, to be in touch with truth we must be in touch with catastrophe. But if the hoped-for transformation of the catastrophic materials is to occur, we must be properly equipped. Properly equipped, for Bion, means that the psyche should be open to the impressions and experiences these materials evoke and should digest them in such a way that they become tolerable, meaningful, and therefore a contribution to the process of growth (I have referred to the necessary mental equipment in Buddhist terms as the combination of awareness and equanimity). Where the alpha function is impaired, so that it fails to turn the components of experience into alpha elements – mental elements that could be described as memory components, which can be stored and used for emotional processing in dream-thoughts or in wakeful conscious or unconscious thinking (Gampel, 2004) – there sense impressions will not undergo transformation. They remain as they are, raw elements that the person does not perceive as phenomena but as things-in-themselves. Such a situation reflects "a state of mind precisely contrasting with that of the scientist who knows he is concerned with phenomena but has not the same certitude that the phenomena have a counterpart of things in themselves" (Bion, 1962, p. 6).

So what we have here is two opposing conditions, each with its own deficiencies. In the first of these, a person misperceives the basic components of her experience as absolute objective reality. Here, there is neither transformation nor representation, signifying registration, nor space for processing or reflection. In the second condition, while being aware of the subjective, relative status of her perceptions (which have undergone transformation and can be thought and dreamed), the person lives nevertheless in a world that has no connection with the absolute truth, with things in themselves. The first condition describes pathological illusion; the second describes the normative illusion of relativism, the illusion of the common citizen. There is, however, for Bion, a third state in which the one whose processing ability is sound and well-developed can achieve contact with O, with infinity, absolute truth, things in themselves. She cannot "know" things in themselves because they are by definition not objects of knowledge; she can, however, intuit O directly, become O. And when O evolves sufficiently to encounter her knowledge (K) capacities – the capacities which allow her to know – then she can point out O (or, more precisely, she can point out its evolution) and formulate it in terms deriving from the domain of sense experience (Bion, 1970).

Contact with the truth requires that experiential elements turn into memory elements. They must become storable (in a container, in memory) for the sake of processing (Bion, 1962, 1970). If, however, this container's activity remains subject to the pleasure principle, directed by the desire for the pleasant and the desire to be rid of the unpleasant, by the wish to appropriate and the impulse to evacuate – then the mind in which the container operates remains dominated by the sensual sphere, which has nothing in common with absolute truth. Knowledge relies on memory (which is also part of knowledge). Memory itself relies on the senses, which, being subject to the pleasure principle, are naturally limited and therefore cause distortion. To formulate the truth, one must rely on memory and desire; but to be in touch with it, to begin with, the mind must be (temporarily) free of them. If there is to be a chance that the other side, who listens to the formulation (in the therapeutic situation: the person seeking therapy), will also make contact with this truth, the formulation itself must be such that it does not arouse memory and desire (Bion, 1970).

And so true knowledge requires a transformation of O into K, while K is ridded of memory and desire: this arises from a state of being-at-one-with the absolute truth (the thing in itself, the unknowable), which cannot be represented by the senses; yet, when it undergoes sufficient evolution, it forms and appears in a field that allows representation and knowledge. In this field representation is unsaturated and K is independent of the pleasure principle, free of memory and desire (Bion, 1970, p. 30–33).

For Bion memory and desire are two sides of one coin: both consist of elements based on sense impressions, and both suggest an absence of immediate sensual gratification. Memory relates to a sense of property, whereas the remembering function is to be considered the container for this property, its storage space. Desire relates to what has yet to be achieved – and this, according to Bion, implies it is still not "saturated"; nevertheless, it has a masking and interfering effect of its own (Bion, 1970). In a Buddhist perspective, the link of "craving" (desire for the pleasant and rejection of the unpleasant) leads directly into the link of "clinging". A clinging hand is a hand that appropriates and is therefore full, stuffed or "saturated", to use Bion's word; so it is obvious why, in Bion's terms, desire is tied to memory and like it obstructs the perception of truth.

Bion seeks to temporarily suspend or suppress memory, desire, and the need to understand. He attempts to achieve control over them, to suppress one function and then another – as if alternatingly covering up the right eye and then the left – to find out how reality looks without them (Bion, 1970). It seems impossible to avoid memory, desire, the need to make sense, and reliance on sense impressions and not to thereby also deny reality, Bion wrote, but what he is after is something that is unlike what's usually considered reality: the psychoanalytic reality, or the emotional reality which can be perceived by means of intuition (Bion, 1970). Bion's absolute truth – O – is clearly more profound than the conventional truth, and it is not the conventional equipment, which yields conventional knowledge, that is required to be in touch with it. Yet the reality Bion considers the absolute truth is not identical to the Buddha's absolute truth, *nibbāna*: *nibbāna* is *nirodha*, absolute cessation, and it is not situated in the domain of mind and matter. Though Bion's truth cannot be perceived by means of the five senses whose objects are the qualities of matter, it is still an object of the mind, and hence part of the world of phenomena (Barnea-Astrog, 2017). So, if we want to draw a line of real commonality between the experiences which these two content areas (psychoanalysis and Buddhism) envision – this must occur on the stratum of insight: the knowledge spontaneously arising in the mental space, which is not fixated, not saturated, and is temporarily free of confusion and desire.

Faith as a scientific state of mind

Let us now go back to the relationship between the catastrophic experience and the possibility to make contact with the truth. In the good case, when the psyche has the capacity to process its raw materials, the sense of catastrophe operates as a signal and enables one to touch life and death – that is, to engage with the processes of creation and destruction from which the sense of catastrophe emerges and at which it points. It therefore enables sensitivity to truth. In other cases the sense of catastrophe becomes distorted and loses its value as signal: either it becomes, for the mind in which it occurs, all of reality, or feeling turns blunt and the mind closes up to it, losing its sensitivity to terror and danger (Eigen, 1985). Culture, Eigen suggested, may well be working in that way on a larger scale: "We lose our sensitivity to our most pressing dangers, much as the toad boils to death without noticing as the heat in its water gradually increases" (Eigen, 1985, p. 329).

A necessary condition for the above-mentioned "good case" is the presence of faith. Bion uses the word *faith* (for which he prescribes the letter F) to denote the state of mind that constitutes the alternative to one dominated by memory and desire. Faith, in this definition, is a condition for becoming O. No faith is required to perceive what can be seen, heard, touched, tasted, or smelled. Faith is relevant only in regard to the existence of a reality not perceived by the mental functions that rely on the senses. Bion's faith is not the same as religious faith: it is what marks the scientific process (Bion, 1970). It is the state of mind shared by "anyone who seeks to know something" (Pelled, 2005, p. 206); to know truly, to know truth, not only what is known through the desiring self. Faith can "save" catastrophe and identify it as a fundamental condition of our being (Eigen, 1985), and this identification is necessary: "To blunt our awareness of catastrophe is to lose or never gain our sensitivity to ourselves" (Eigen, 1985, p. 329). Awareness of catastrophe is sensitivity to ourselves. Awareness of suffering as a characteristic of existence is sensitivity to ourselves, to reality, to the world. This is what Eigen wrote:

> One opens oneself to reality (O) not because the latter is good or bad – it may be both and neither – but because it is. [. . .] Faith is an open attitude that lets things register. It is not the closed faith of a particular religious dogma, ready to do violence to what is outside it. The faith Bion has in mind is part of the need sensitivity has to taste life, to feel impacts and digest them in ways that lead to more life.
>
> (2004, p. 9)

Not because it is good or bad – that is, in a manner that is not subject to the pleasure principle. Needing to feel impacts, even at the price of vulnerability – that is, openness to experience and the experience of sensitivity are expressions of mental growth and contact with life.

> This kind of faith is an attempt not to do violence to experience, an attempt that must fail, perhaps. But the attitude it embodies is significant – a caring, devotion, sincerity, respect, an imaginative loving objectivity, a drive to do life justice, a need to do right by experience. If taken seriously, one possible result of this kind of faith is increased ability to wait on each other, wait for each other [. . .]. It is a faith that comes back for more, that keeps opening and opening in the face of trauma waves, that registers impacts and learns to work with them.
>
> (Eigen, 2004, pp. 9–10).

Faith faces the truth nakedly. Whether or not it is pleasant, whether or not it is familiar – faith is willing to receive it. The truth of catastrophe, of disintegration, of fragmentation. The truth of impermanence, of suffering, of the absent essential self. Realizing the truth leads to nonviolent actions. Openness to it, a priori, represents the ethical position of gentleness.

Saddhā: *sober faith*

In the Buddha's teaching, the mental factor of faith, trust, or confidence is called *saddhā*. Faith in the Buddha is confidence in the one who has become completely liberated from ignorance, craving, and hatred; who found out the way to achieve this and, out of infinite compassion, explained it to anyone who wanted to hear. Faith in *Dhamma* is confidence in this truth that he rediscovered: the nature of things and the way to be set free from blindness and suffering. Faith in *Sangha* is confidence in all those who went far enough along this way, investigated the field of arising phenomena in depth, experienced what is beyond it (the cessation of becoming, *nibbāna*) and attained at least the first level of liberation on the way to full enlightenment. Surrender to these three factors is called "taking refuge".

As one walks the eightfold path, the path that leads into the depths of the mind, one finds refuge in the Buddha, in *Dhamma*, and in *Sangha*. He commits himself to their safety; his life itself he puts into their hands. While the path is straight and clear, the depths of his mind still meander, still foggy here and there. He is bound to be confused by the forces that are active there, and they may conceal the path or obstruct it. For this not to take over, he needs proper instruction and protection. What type of protection can he find in these three factors? What kind of refuge do they offer, what shelter? And how do this type of faith and surrender relate to the scientific state of mind and the sober investigation of reality?

Not everyone who calls himself a Buddhist or a devotee of the Buddha, the *Dhamma*, and the *Saṅgha* practices the main part of what the Buddha taught: the part of meditation, of the cultivation of the mind and the dissolution of its harmful residues. I am referring to those who do follow this path – or consider following it – and practice its principles to the best of their abilities. For them the nature of faith and its objects must be carefully distinct. The path, as said (see Chapter 2), consists of three aspects: "right" behavior, right concentration, and wisdom or a realistic view. The meditation practice develops both right concentration and wisdom and brings together, inseparably, elements of calmness, control, and strength on the one hand, and of close, investigative attention that seeks to be non-biased and non-reactive on the other. At the same time, all three aspects of the path lead into and support one another, and the aspect of wisdom follows directly from meditation, which itself must be directed by a necessary minimum of right view. Let us touch upon these three aspects and see what role faith plays in each.

Control and strength are required to direct oneself to moral action and to change harmful habits. Like a wild, untamed beast that goes berserk in a crowded marketplace, there is nothing more destructive than the wild mind doing whatever occurs to it. Like a well-trained strong animal, there is nothing more useful: obedient and disciplined, it lets itself be enlisted for good action (Goenka, 2004). Faith is one of the five positive faculties that can rule the mind, and one of the five forces that can firmly and fearlessly overcome the psyche's reluctance to direct itself towards the good (Ledi Sayadaw, 2009). The remaining four are effort, awareness, concentration, and wisdom.[4] Faith, as a ruling factor and as an overpowering force, operates on two levels. On the first level[5] it is the germ of every pure action, of moral behavior and generosity. Without it, the mind will naturally tend to take pleasure from impure actions only (ibid.). Given its default options and its archaic inclinations, it is easier for the mind to lash out in a rage against someone who hurt us than to stop and examine the situation carefully. It is both more predictable and primitive for one to get egotistic pleasure from sensual delights than it is to find happiness through serving one's fellow humans. The first level of faith directs us to aim for a more ethical mode of conduct, which is why it is a necessary factor. This, however, does not suffice to gain a hold on the mind and to stabilize it fundamentally and for the long run.

Another level of faith,[6] one that evolves from practice, is required to affect deeper layers of the mind. Here, as it accompanies meditation, faith prepares the grounds for the mind's true strength. It represents, in this context, the eclipse of fluctuating, distracted attention and the emergence of the stable and clear mind. Then attention can focus uninterruptedly on the objects of its meditation. If the mind succeeds in focusing in this manner – for instance, on the incoming breath and the outgoing breath in the systematic practice of awareness to breathing,[7] as it is described in the category "observation of the body", one of the four bases of awareness (satipṭṭhāna) – then the deep level of faith as a ruling principle is attained. Moreover, as long as faith is subject to craving, it cannot overcome one's destructive mental forces. As fluctuation and distraction dissipate, faith becomes a force that can overcome them (Ledi Sayadaw, 2009). Gradually the screen of desire and hatred lifts, the screen of dullness and laziness, the screen of restlessness and doubt. All these wear off and grow weak, becoming distinct as objects of examination in themselves; below them, radiantly, wisdom appears.

Provided the meditator has the benefit of a sufficient basic understanding, instructing him to practice in an intelligent way, a process of disillusion and liberation will get underway. Again and again, this process passes through awareness of the true nature of things, their arising and fading away, the manner in which suffering comes about and the manner in which it can be exhausted. Between the habitual process of emergence of suffering and its interruption, the connecting link is faith:

> Ignorance is the supporting condition for mental reactions [and the habitual patterns they form]. Reactions [and the habitual patterns they form] are the supporting condition for consciousness. Consciousness is the supporting condition for [the] mind-and-matter [phenomenon]. [The] mind-and-matter [phenomenon] is the supporting condition for the six sense spheres. The six sense spheres are the supporting condition for contact [with mental and material objects]. Contact [with mental and material objects] is the supporting condition for sensation. Sensation is the supporting condition for craving [and aversion]. Craving [and aversion] is the supporting condition for clinging. Clinging is the supporting condition for [the process of] becoming. [The process of] becoming is the supporting condition for birth. Birth is the supporting condition for suffering, for painful states.
>
> (SN 12.23)

Thus far the chain of *saṃsāra*. From here, emancipation:

> Suffering is the supporting condition for faith. Faith is the support-
> ing condition for joy. Joy is the supporting condition for rapture.[8]
> Rapture is the supporting condition for tranquility. Tranquility is the
> supporting condition for pleasant states. Pleasant states are the sup-
> porting condition for concentration. Concentration is the support-
> ing condition for the knowledge of seeing things as they are. The
> knowledge of seeing things as they are is the supporting condition
> for disenchantment. Disenchantment is the supporting condition for
> dispassion. Dispassion is the supporting condition for liberation.
> Liberation is the supporting condition for the knowledge of eradica-
> tion [of all mental defilements].
>
> (SN 12.23)

Like the rain falling on the mountain top – when the cracks, the conduits,
and the gorges fill up with water, it flows on to fill the pools; once the
pools are filled, the water continues down into the lakes, and then into
the streams, from which it flows into the rivers; once the water has filled
the rivers, it flows into the ocean – in the same way, each of the above
conditions, when it is fulfilled, leads to the next (SN 12.23). The emergence of faith, in this formulation, relies on suffering. From suffering
springs faith.

We all know a certain strain of faith that flourishes from suffering:
distress, despair, and fear, when shrouded in ignorance, lead many people to cling to all kinds of elements: gods, leaders, ideas, customs, the
products of their projections and split-off self-parts – to which they turn
in their perplexity to feel safe. The most immediate association we have
for the word *faith* is with religion, and with the word *blind* – and this fits
the above-mentioned strain. But the faith the Buddha referred to, which,
as said, links the process whereby suffering arises and the process of
release from it, is situated in a different domain. Similar to Bion's notion
of faith, it touches upon openness to truth and therefore does not clash
with the spirit of investigation. The faith that a Buddha aims for must be
founded on understanding, and the meditator should question anything
that deserves to be questioned and thoroughly examine the objects of
his faith. At the same time, however, we are told that doubt is one of the
basic causes of delusion. How do we draw the line between what we
should trust and what we must doubt; between the doubt that allows us
to reach the truth and that which conceals it? This is the big question,
and it can only be answered as one makes the essential passage from

the intellectual level to the experiential one. There the following relationship gradually transpires: Wisdom and faith are complementary and keep each other in balance. Wisdom directs faith to the right place, and faith allows work and progress without doubt interfering and undermining the process, tripping one at every other step. Faith, trust, confidence, and surrender must turn to objects that have been identified by wisdom and clear vision as worthy (Nyanatiloka, 1997). Worthy objects lead to release from the shackles of ignorance, desire, and hatred; that is to say, they lead to liberation from the factors whose dissolving is the condition for seeing reality-as-it-is.

The mental factor "faith" emerges and grows from suffering. This, however, is not tantamount to stating that we must deliberately cause ourselves to suffer. Existence in this life naturally entails suffering, and we must acknowledge this and identify suffering in its diverse manifestations, even where it is cloaked in a transient veil of pleasure. If it is intelligent and not blind, faith involves contact with the truth; the identification of impermanence and pleasure as derivatives of the field of suffering is an integral part of the process of dispelling illusion. The refuge offered by this type of faith is a refuge that exposes reality rather than occluding it, and the protection it provides is of the kind that can only be offered by the path leading to total liberation: protection from our own self-destructiveness, originating in our own stock of mental defilements.

Sober faith helps us grow stable and devote ourselves to practice that reveals the nature of reality. And once we are aware that change, disintegration, separation, and suffering are features of existence itself, it assists us not to be crushed by terror and despair. Together with the other interrelating factors, faith accompanies us through realization of the noble truths regarding suffering and its emergence, to the realization of the noble truths regarding the cessation of suffering and the way that leads there.

Holding and surrender

Faith in the Buddhist sense of the word is related to stability of mind, and the capacity of attention to focus undistractedly on its appropriate object is a manifestation of well-established faith. This being the case, we might expect that the mind of those whose faith is as yet underdeveloped will fluctuate.

I would not venture to claim that anyone whose mind fluctuates lacks sufficiently developed faith, and certainly not that anyone whose mind is focused on her object of meditation has profoundly grounded faith as defined by the Buddha. I want to be cautious here, for one category of cases does not necessarily tell us about all. The dynamics we are looking at embrace many factors, and I am far from able to fully cover them. For now, what I can say is that the degree to which the mind does or does not succeed in focusing exclusively on its chosen meditation object is *also* related to the foundation of faith, but no less to the nature of the meditation object and to other characteristics of the person who meditates. As concerns the object of meditation, it seems easier to keep focused on "external" objects, like a sound or a shape in the surroundings, or on "constructed" objects, like a sound or shape that have been internalized, a mantra, an image, or a likeness, than it is to stay focused on a natural object that requires inward-directed observation, like for instance body sensations or breathing as they naturally occur – sensations and breathing as they are. With regard to the person's own characteristics, there are complex interrelations between positive factors and skillful abilities that have developed in the person, to a greater or lesser extent, and violent and deceptive elements that have accumulated within her, to a greater or lesser extent, and then were dissolved, more or less; and these join together from one moment to the next and influence the process, which never comes to rest. I don't wish, at this point, to approach all these. The following thoughts, rather, I will devote to the relations between faith and mental stability. In our particular discussion concerning the fundamental experience of being a gentle person who longs to feel held in the world, it seems to me that this relationship, setting aside my reservations, opens up an interesting field for investigation.

Let us revert to the three forms of self-holding, three formations of second skin that serve the self as a way of surviving in the face of the dread of un-integration. In the case of infants, these are focus on a sensory object, muscular tension or contraction, and constant motion. These may continue into adulthood, taking various shapes, including less physical, more mental versions. Such a mental version can be the intense focus on an internal or external object, immersing oneself in it, holding onto it by means of attention, and therefore get a sense of being held. Or one can adhere to certain experiences or ideas, contract oneself around them and use them as anchors that give a sense of solidity. Or one can be in incessant mental movement, not leaving spaces in the stream of images and thoughts, so as to feel continuous and uninterrupted. It is very likely that if a person at the earliest stages of life had to use these mechanisms massively, they will go along with her into adult life, at least to some extent. If this person should start practicing meditation using natural, internal objects, it is also very likely that the mechanisms she developed, together with the suffering and constraint they compile, will make themselves known to her all the more forcefully.

In the case of one person, it is constant inner movement that takes the upper hand. His mind does not stand still, leaping from thought to idea to memory to feeling. He finds it extremely hard to stay focused on the object of meditation. Though he works patiently, bringing his attention back to his incoming and outgoing breath, for example, or to the systematic scan of his bodily sensations, it's an uphill struggle, and it may stay that way for many long years. Another person's mind may tend to take tight hold of its objects. She is in the habit of sticking to them, internally, elaborating and thickening them by means of tendentious processes of evaluation and labeling, which have a certain impact on her sense of self, and she clings to them with all her might. She too will find it hard to stay with her meditation object: hard to remove her attention from where it is so forcefully tied, from the place to which she is accustomed. One can largely say that these two behaviors, to some extent, occur in every person, and therefore in every meditator (especially at the early stages, and in unquiet, stormy times). After all, they reflect universal habitual tendencies of the untrained mind. But in the case of this man and this woman and their likes, these habits are sometimes especially stubbornly rooted.

In yet another case, where the archaic survival-oriented mechanism involves focus on a sense object (internal or external), focus on the meditation object may become compromised because this primary object is competing for its place at the center of attention (as in the second case of tightening and clinging). This might, on the other hand, assist the meditator in fixing his attention on the object of meditation: he is used to immersing his attention in an object, setting all else aside. But it is exactly for this reason that this might result in masking the disturbance: this person is used to getting immersed in some chosen object while detaching himself from the rest of the world. His meditation practice can get hooked up to this defensive tendency and collude with it, and in the absence of proper guidance and understanding, this might keep reality concealed from him rather than helping him penetrate it.

Non-violent control of the mind and the ability to focus on a natural, internal object require surrender and faith, and when this control and focus are well developed, this is a sign that faith and the ability to surrender are established. Restless movement and clinging are basic features of the untrained mind, the regular behaviors which, having been repeated countlessly many times, have become entrenched. Sometimes the restless mind, the contracting-clinging mind, or the immersing-disconnecting mind have come to be this way because their respective early reality (whether concrete or in fantasy) communicated to their owners that there was no one to rely on. These mechanisms, however, having emerged and fulfilled their purpose for the self's survival, go on interfering with the ability to let go, surrender, and have a full experience of trust.

Trusting oneself is as important as trusting the path and the person who guides one on that path. I must be confident of the path itself: know that it is beneficial and not harmful, that it is straight and not crooked, that it is intelligible and clear and doesn't lead to a dead end, that it leads to true liberation and doesn't misguide me. I must trust those who show me the path: know that they are moral people, free of personal interests (with regard to their teaching), and that they teach from pure compassion; that they have progressed far enough to develop wisdom and a clear view of things, and to be very familiar with the process of shedding accumulations of ignorance, desire, and hatred. I must similarly also trust myself: i.e., believe I have the ability to understand the path and to follow it. There is, however, a difference between this confidence in the self's ability to understand the path and to follow it, and unbalanced self-reliance, which entails, among other things, holding mechanisms used in a rigid and generalized manner. The first refers to someone who sees that she also has to rely on others – appropriate, deserving others who have been carefully and consciously selected. She understands that the focus of responsibility is inside her and that no one can take over her job in this sense; but also that her mind is limited and in need of useful interaction and instruction, or else she will be forever stuck in her own world. The second refers to one who finds it hard to receive help: either she erroneously assumes that she can manage alone, and that there is no other way (an illusion not only supported by personality traits; it also has cultural underpinnings), or the more adult layers of her psyche reach out to appropriate others, while more primitive layers continue to hold themselves by themselves, not confident enough to let go and commit themselves, however briefly, to what they perceive as extraneous.

Vipassana meditation, as S. N. Goenka teaches it, typically involves the systematic movement (as opposed to the restless, erratic movement mentioned earlier) of attention from one area of the body to another. This type of movement, when it is accompanied by "right view" or proper mental attitude, serves to develop awareness and equanimity towards the entire field of sensations. This movement of attention expresses, on the one hand, a thorough observation of the mental-material phenomenon, and on the other, non-clinging. Non-clinging is necessary for systematic movement: when a sensation is pleasant, one is tempted to linger and enjoy it. This leads to attachment or clinging. When the sensation is unpleasant, there is a temptation to withdraw and escape, or on the contrary, to dwell on it and develop a negative mental attitude to it – two additional behaviors defined as clinging. This movement is not always smooth: sometimes it is necessary to rest the attention on a vague area or one in which there is no awareness of sensation. Still, movement is systematic and continuous, and for this to be the case, a sufficient degree of control of the mind is required. When the mind is unable to move continuously, when it insists on getting stuck somewhere and clinging to it, or when it scatters every which way, losing itself, jumping from one thing to the next as thoughts take up a considerable slice of attention and prevent focusing on the meditation object – what is it, really, that interferes with its conscious intention? Why can't the mind keep moving, surrender fully to its initial, chosen action? A force of habit, mainly: the manifestation of certain negative mental accumulations and of certain insufficiently developed positive factors. And perhaps, by way of a secondary category, also a specific instance of the above: the mind is unable to surrender because it lacks trust or faith. Perhaps, even though in-depth processes have already enabled it to develop trust in people, in the path, in a good teacher, and in its own competence, more primitive layers still carry residues of distrust that prevent it from letting go of the self-holding mechanisms, and these interfere with the mind's ability to focus and relax and prevent it from moving systematically without becoming either scattered or hooked.

The factors involved in determining the course of the meditative process are many and complex, as said, and it may not be useful to try and unravel them. Often it may even be detrimental. One commonly accepted category to approach a few of these factors is that of *nīvarana*, the five mental obstacles, the veils that conceal the truth. These are, as mentioned, sensual desire; hatred and malice; laziness, drowsiness, and dullness; restlessness and worry; and skeptic doubt. These prevent a person from seeing reality clearly and from distinguishing between what is good and what is bad for her and others; and in the presence of any of these five, neither a high level nor even a moderate level of concentration can be attained (Nyanatiloka, 1997). *Nīvarana* is a useful category. It is useful to be aware that "right now there is restlessness in my mind or nervousness or concern". It is useful to be aware that "now there is doubt in my mind", or "hatred", or "laziness", or "lust". Awareness of the presence or absence of these factors at any given moment in time is part of the observation of the mind's contents, the fourth part of practicing the establishment of awareness, *satipṭṭhāna*. It is less useful, and possibly even distracting, in the context of meditation, to try and interpret the mind's behavior and to understand why this or that worry, hatred, or doubt make their appearance now, and what in one's personal history might have produced them. In this sense, this discussion of mine is treading a fine line and might even be tripping over it: When one takes the psychodynamic perspective in studying the mind, the thought that this tendency towards restless inner movement or this tendency to forcefully cling to an object is the outcome of early experiences with early objects is supposed to cast light on habitual mental behaviors and encourage insight. But in the context of meditation, this very same thought is bound to constitute mental subject matter that may distract from the main task, and worse, it may lead to erroneous labeling of a present reality, causing a chain of reactions that, rather than undoing the causes of suffering, will only add to them. There is therefore a certain clash between these two levels of investigation, as they have different aims and approach them in different ways. The personal-subjective level and the universal one require different treatments. Yet they are connected: it could not be otherwise, as both exist in reality and express it.

I suggested earlier that one of the lines stretching between the respective experiences that the two theories of mind (psychodynamic and Buddhist) have in view is situated in the deep stratum of insight: the knowledge that arises spontaneously as a result of experience occurring in a mental space that is non-clinging, non-saturated, and temporarily free of confusion and desire. The insight that Bion's F in O reaches is gained without effort, without appropriation of, or greed for, the truth. The "selected fact"[9] presents itself from among the mess of facts; the connection flashes up and emerges intuitively; coherence appears out of chaos and ambiguity. Insights arising in the mind of the meditator, too, come to her without her making any appeal. She practices in her particular way, and while she does so, she doesn't engage in an interpretive-intellectual inquiry. But in the course of her practice, her mental layers open and reveal themselves to her: components and patterns present themselves from the medley of particles of experience, connections flash up and arise intuitively, coherence emerges from chaos and ambiguity.

Overly intense investment in interpretation and etiology is likely to hamper the meditator, and insights about her personal history are not the point of the Buddha's ways of practice – they are secondary fruits that ripen in the course of it. The personal-subjective stratum and the universal one have a way of occluding one another (right eye covered; left eye covered; both covered; neither), but they also render account of one another at times. The universal is valid for the personal-subjective; the personal-subjective always derives from a broader rule: it is a specific instance, and when observed from the right angle, it points at that rule.

Let us, then, go on considering our specific instance: If the meditator is capable in the course of meditation of resigning her mental activities and the other mental contents that preoccupy her at a certain moment, then she can successfully focus on the meditation object. If she relies too heavily on these activities and contents for the sake of survival, or if for some other reasons her attraction and attachment to them is overly strong, they will continue vying for her attention, split and distract it. When thinking about the mechanisms the self adopts to survive, we are largely dealing with psychological etiology, interpretations of history. But this thinking might also take us one step further into the realm of universal truth. If we are ready, while we experientially analyze ourselves, to see the deeper sense of the phenomenon, we might be able to discern this: The mind depends on its actions, its reactions, its movements and attachments for its continued existence. It is, in other words, dependent on them for its survival. From *saṅkhāra* arises *viññāṇa*: it is from mental reactions, mental habits, deep-rooted tendencies, the residues of past actions that have become engraved as patterns of mental behavior – from all this flows consciousness, that which we experience as the internal space that differentiates the self from what it experiences as external to it, that which produces us as subjects. From *upādāna* arises *bhava*: it is through our attachments and clinging that we come into being.

The self makes a great effort to maintain itself, to survive, to continue. Consciousness continues for as long as there are reactive residues to feed it. Coming into being occurs for as long as we cling. We survive and continue: in a sense this is an achievement; in another, the achievement isn't enough. By means of these mechanisms we advance to a level of normative suffering (*dukkha*), and, circumstances allowing, to a level of suffering that pushes the well-enough mind to seek a way out, to act energetically to be released from its constraints. We survive, we continue, but becoming itself is suffering. We hold on tight and ostensibly we don't fall apart, but each moment of clinging is a moment of coming into being in an existence stamped with separation, devastation, and decay.

Non-clinging

To learn from experience, to grow and become free, a person must be able to put himself in a space in which true knowledge emerges as a result of non-clinging to knowledge. He must surrender himself to processes on which he has very little grip. Of course he is always there anyway, in the midst of processes that are beyond his control, but he must be able to acknowledge this and let go – however briefly, however deficiently – of his attempts to control, of the desperate need to hold and cling. How is one who, due to a composite of internal and external factors, was unable to experience good-enough holding – the kind of holding that is the very groundwork of trust – to lend faith to anything beyond herself, to put herself in its hands and trust it will hold her adequately? And how can we, all of us, feel held in a world that prompts us to shed any illusion of solidity and permanence? How can we surrender ourselves, open-eyed, to processes which we might recognize as being helpful but over which we have no control? How can this person, whose body's tiniest cell is inhabited by a sense of catastrophe, transform catastrophe so as to be in touch with herself and the world in a life-giving way? And how can we all open ourselves to the truths of suffering and impermanence to reach, thereby, what is free of suffering, free of dread?

Bion says: The emotional state of transformation in O, when memory, desire, and understanding are suspended, is a lonely and fearful state:

> Like one that on a lonesome road
> Doth walk in fear and dread;
> And having once turned round walks on,
> And turns no more his head;
> Because he knows a frightful fiend
> Doth close behind him tread.
> (Coleridge, in: Bion, 1970, p. 46)

The Buddha says: In states of extreme terror, remember me, the *Dhamma*, or the *Saṅgha*:

> Whether gone to the forest, to the root of A tree or dwelling
>   in an empty space,
> You should remember the Sammasambuddha,
> And whatever fear you behold will pass away.
> If you do not recall the Buddha,
> The highest in the world, the foremost of men
> Then you should remember the Dhamma,
> Leading to salvation, so well explained.
> But if you don't recall the Dhamma,
> Leading to salvation, so well explained,

Then remember the Saṅgha,
This endless field of merit
Fear, stupefaction and your hairs standing on end will no more be.
(SN 11.3. In: Nothnagel, 2015)

Coleridge's frightful fiend, which Bion mentioned, is both the search for truth and the active defenses against it. As for the quote of the Buddha's instructions, it would be reasonable for us to wonder: Being a part of a doctrine based on full personal responsibility, the investigation of reality, and the breakdown of illusions, how can reliance on external factors be of real profit? The Buddha explains: In times of distress and fear, if someone raises his eyes towards the name or figure of a leader, no matter how powerful and elevated, this will either help him or not. The Buddha mentions a historic battle in which the great leader tried to encourage the fighters by suggesting they should look up at his flag and remember him or one of three other kings whenever they felt fear, experienced terror, their hairs standing on end. But alas, the fighters lost the battle. They lost, explains the Buddha, because they attempted to derive strength and solace from factors unfree of ignorance, craving, and hatred, and one who is not free of ignorance, craving, and hatred is not free of fear either. However, he tells the meditators, if in the course of their meditation they must do battle with their inner enemies and are struck by terror, then their faith in factors that are free of ignorance, craving, and hatred – and hence of fear – will protect and support them. Fear, bewilderment, and hair-raising dread will no longer be their lot (SN 11.3).

One who tries to follow the Buddha's path tells himself from time to time, "I take refuge in the Buddha, I take refuge in the *Dhamma*, I take refuge in the *Saṅgha*. I put my safety with them, I find shelter in them, I put my very life in their hands". On the face of it, this appears to be a simple act of religious faith; but faith can be either blind or with eyes wide open (religious or non-religious – that would be a matter of definition). So, in the name of sobriety, let us have a closer look and ask: Does he find shelter with a private person, a rigid paradigm, a community that blindly obeys a closed system of injunctions, rules, and customs? Does he find shelter with certain essential entities that detach him from reality? With a supreme power that saves him, seemingly, from the consequences of his own actions? With a false sense of knowledge that hides him away from the truth? If this is the case, then taking refuge loses its original beneficial properties. The struggle of one who follows the path is an internal struggle against one's negative mental accumulations, and the objects to which he lifts his gaze, too, are to a large extent internal. What truly offers support is the *qualities* of these objects (Buddha, *Dhamma*, *Saṅgha*): qualities which the meditator identifies in these external factors, in others – and then practices with the aim of fostering them in himself. These external factors, these objects of faith, are not sectarian either. "Buddha", rather than being the name of a private person, aggrandizing himself as if he were the best among men, is an adjective representing the qualities of awakening, liberation, lucidity, and enlightenment (therefore *the* or *a* precedes *Buddha*: "the awakened", "the enlightened", "a fully liberated one"). Siddhattha Gotama, the private person who came to be a Buddha, wasn't the first to become a Buddha, nor is he expected to be the last. The *Dhamma*, rather than being a religion, institution or dogma, is a way of representing the qualities of the investigation of truth and the liberation from the bondage of illusion. The *Saṅgha* is not a religious order, but a group of people embodying qualities of purity, nobility of mind, and awakening. When I find shelter with them, I am not hiding: I look for cover among qualities whose nature is revelation and exposure. When I find refuge there, I'm not supposed to cling: I am held by qualities whose nature is non-clinging. In turning to them, I am saved by qualities I must foster in myself through years of diligent work, qualities that puncture the illusion of solidity and the false beliefs that construe a permanent and essential self – as well as an external, permanent, and essential element that can deliver this self.

Devotion, surrender, and faith are all potentially beautiful qualities. It is the mental intention at their roots and the objects to which they address themselves that determine what fruits they bear. If the object is a construction, the product of anxiety or laziness or dullness or neglect, then the fruit of surrender and faith is not the same as when the object is the removal of the shackles of ignorance, hatred, and desire by means of penetrating analysis. If the underlying intention is the denial of reality and the renouncement of responsibility, then the fate of surrender and faith is not the same as when the investigation of truth and the movement towards gentleness are envisioned. Faith that relies on a projective state of mind is blind faith, a faith that hides. Open-eyed faith expresses openness to the truth. The first leads to violence against what it perceives as foreign to itself. The second leads to the identification of suffering as a universal feature of existence, and as a result, to a sense of companionship, compassion, and love.

Dwelling in the unsettled space of not-knowing

"Knowledge 'about' something may be the outcome of a defence against the consequences of an 'act of faith'", said Bion (1970, p. 35). The act of faith allows the mind to let go even in less-than-comfortable situations, to open its ranks and crack so that truth can break forth. Those who are able to tolerate gaps in their mind's reactivity and do not have a need to fill them up immediately – those who can cope with a sense of imper-manence, a lack of solidity and essence, and avoid contracting their self into a small, tight ball as soon as these arise – have the capacity to not defend themselves rigidly against the act of faith, which is imbued with openness, sensitivity, and gentleness in the first place.

This is what Bion wrote about the state of mind in which this process takes place.

> The sense of loneliness seems to relate to a feeling, in the object of scrutiny, that it is being abandoned and, in the scrutinizing sub-ject, that it is cutting itself off from the source or base on which it depends for its existence. [. . .] Detachment can only be achieved at the cost of painful feelings of loneliness and abandonment [. . .]. The "detached" personality is in a sense new to its job and has to turn to tasks which differ from those to which its components are more usually adapted, namely scrutiny of the environment excluding the self; part of the price paid is in feelings of insecurity.
>
> (Bion, 1963, pp. 15–16)

What happens in a space where not-knowing and non-clinging are active in the event a self-part – an idea, intellectual paradigm, worldview, fun-damental feeling – encounters a reality that destabilizes it and is con-sequently abandoned? The abstract vignette below contemplates the qualities of this not-so-simple experience. It demonstrates how it relates to fear, loneliness, and insecurity – yet no less to faith, surrender, open-ness to truth and non-violence with regard to experience.

***

This is what happened – not for the first time, and surely it will not be the last: reality patted me on the shoulder and proved me wrong. It feels nice to know, to luxuriate in a downy good sense of self. But as it happened, this soft grounding was no longer, and I found myself helplessly looking on as it faded, scattering every which way, vanishing into space.

I try to acknowledge what's happening, not to turn my back to it. To allow it to crack an opening in me, to enter my world of inner structures and have its way.

First it encounters the battered structure. The structure is torn from its roots, which were hitherto stuck in the self, and loses its habitual status. Now, with what remains of its severed arms, it has to feel its way to a new site in which it can strike anchor – else it will be lost forever. Meanwhile it drifts in the mind's space, uprooted, neither swallowed nor ejected, strange and familiar at once, the ordinary that has become uncanny. On its way it passes other bodies, touching and not touching them, radiating its present qualities onto them. In its strange light, they too suddenly appear less familiar, less easy to identify with. The mind eyes them cautiously, suspicious – no longer certain of anything. It is unsure of the nature of these bodies, of their status and value. It does not trust its own perception, its ability to properly discern.

If the severed structure was big enough, it will also unsettle other structures, shaking up or loosening their links to the self. If the area from which it was torn is large or deep enough, then the vacuum will suck its surroundings into it and transform them.

What to do about this self, whose imaginary face has changed? What to do with this inner space when the bodies constituting it have lost their grip on the self, or when this grip has grown fickle and faint? What to do with these self-parts, which the mind tries to tie and stitch back together, without much success? What to do with this yearning, the wish to feel the old, cozy familiarity, the ongoing sense of a good self? What to do with this suspiciousness and insecurity, with the loss of faith?

I maintain the external shape and wait for the internal space to rearrange itself.

On the stage, playing:

1   Clinging to the pleasantness that was, and hoping it will return.
2   Desire for experience beyond experience, what is not of this world, what emerged in the past when familiar structures broke down. Desire for experience beyond experience, what is not of this world and has never been experienced before. A sly desire, one that appears smilingly each time the mind notes a crack in knowledge, an opening to strangeness. A desire which, before anything, demolishes the very thing it covets.
3   Doubt, a devouring mouth, a hidden hand that voids all meaning from anything stable, obvious, and safe.

Bion says: the emotional state of transformation in O, the suspension of memory, desire, and understanding, is a state of loneliness and dread. The Buddha says: if in the process of mental purification through meditation, some horrible contents rise to the surface and your hair stands on end – then remember me, the *Dhamma*, or the *Saṅgha*.

I maintain the external shape and wait for the internal space to rearrange itself.

I try to allow all components of experience to arise and to pass at their own pace, and not to be carried away by 1, 2, or 3. I try to allow them to drift, to express the combination of factors that created them (the past) and caused them to become manifest (in the present) – until they will have exhausted their current features and be swept away into something else, which will feed another moment of consciousness, which will then feed another constellation of events (the future). I try not to be tempted by a pleasantness awaiting me elsewhere, not to be squashed by unpleasantness. To keep trust while losing faith, trust related to the knowledge of impermanence.

The self strains to reconstruct its identity. The self is built from pleasant experiences. Now it recognizes pleasantness-kindling events and tries to rebuild itself from them. A sense of pleasantness that accompanies clarification and coherence offers it safe ground. But this ground is drifting; it is not sound.

If gentleness develops and matures, sensitivity to subtleties and a moral, non-violent attitude towards them, too, develop. If gentleness develops and matures, the mind identifies the turmoil, the devastation and rupture, the clinging and the sly, demolishing desire. The gnawing doubt, the self that tries to be rebuilt, the temptation, the danger. The drifting ground, the motion of the hand reaching out to hold when it lacks holding. If gentleness develops and matures, it allows all of these to live. If it is able to allow all of these to live, it continues to develop and mature.

The mind seeks to weave itself a narrative. I interrupt it; I don't want to let it soothe and close, I want to be able to slide between the spaces. The mind attempts to re-collect its scatterings, to heap back together a downy nest, impose reason and order. To weave itself a narrative – that is, a thread that stitches together the continuity of self: this and this I was, this and this happened, this and this I have now come to be. A thread that makes the self feel that it exists and that it is good. To impose reason and order – that is, to reconnect the flailing arms of the uprooted structure, or to build another structure, one that seems sufficiently familiar, in its stead.

Underneath the narrative, organization, and order I notice a pleasantness, to which the mind is attracted. Underneath the not-knowing I sense unpleasantness, which the mind repels.

Not-knowing and loss of balance may also feel pleasant, like being afloat. But this is not the case at this moment. At this moment they are associated with shame, a bad sense of self.

I try not to fall on either side, I try to stay tuned to zero. Not to incline towards the pleasant, and not to push away the unpleasant. Any temporary composition that starts to solidify is attended by pleasantness, but it is immediately followed by distrust that undermines it. The composition and solidification lose their status and can no longer serve as shelter. I am a stranger, homeless. I am disintegrating in a disintegrating world.

The narrative does not build. It comes together and crumbles, comes together and crumbles, it does not hold, does not convince. Maybe this, then, is the narrative now – it occurs to me. And then it too disappears.

I am the offspring of moments

when the constrictions of my ignorance and beliefs were eliminated by contrary evidence

moments when my psychological worldview opened

into unrestricted, inconclusive questions and exploration
-(following Fleischman, 2013, p. 320).

I take refuge in Buddha, I take refuge in *Dhamma*, I take refuge in *Sangha*. I have no other refuge but the Buddha, I have no other refuge but the *Dhamma*, I have no other refuge but the *Sangha*.[10] I have faith in everything, I have faith in nothing. There is no faith in me for everything, there is no faith in me for nothing. There is no no-faith in me for everything, there is no no-faith in me for nothing. I trust this moment though it bears no faith. I lean against a no-wall, I stand on ground that has given way.

Hours

Days

Weeks

Slowly the haze of delusion lifts, which the uprooted structure produced before being torn from its origins and abandoned. The delusion created by the rupture itself, too, grows faint and weak. The personality, new to its job, directs itself at different tasks than the ones to which it was hitherto accustomed. My sense of self and experience of the world, having turned away from what they were, flow in a different track. A slightly different feeling in a slightly different world. Another small shift whose place and role in the greater process I still don't know.

Loneliness, anxiety, and alienation gradually dissolve. Elements of experience arise and disappear, break down incessantly, scatter and grow distant, open gaps to fall through. I feel at home in the universe once more.

***

The sense of catastrophe is tied to the element of distance. It is an emotional trace signaling, on the one hand, the emergence of the self, and on the other, the realization that it is a perishing, disintegrating, inessential phenomenon. Fear, loneliness, and insecurity are likely to arise when illusions regarding the permanence and continuity of the self shatter. Faith is needed to maintain openness to truth when circumstances are troubling. The type of faith and its objects must be carefully examined and selected so they can join other mental forces and properly carry out their work. The work is that of liberation from illusion: the illusion of splitting and separation, and the illusion of merging and of fusion.

From everywhere the truth of impermanence, of suffering, and of the absence of essential selfhood turns up: from the personal and from the universal, from the mental and from the material, from the inner universe and from the outer universe. Once we understand ourselves as being products of the universe, as features and manifestations of it and of processes occurring within it (Fleischman, 2013), the investigation of ourselves and the investigation of the universe stand revealed as inextricably bound together. While the element of distance remains undeniable, the split between inside and outside wanes and inward-directed observation loses its narcissistic and egoistic attributes.

I investigate the nature of my mind-and-body because that is my responsibility as a human. I study the nature of my mind-and-body, and in doing so I study the world. I live in this world as a product and manifestation of it. "I" live a very specific life, but the materials out of which I am made up, the laws that regulate the processes taking place "inside me", the unique, constantly changing composition that creates me, the momentary, incessant stream of arising and fading away – all are world, all *loka*. "I" live a specific life and "my" experience is the most personal thing possible; and still, it isn't personal at all. Specificity and universality are not mutually exclusive: specificity is universal in nature. If this is how we see things, we can feel at home in an ever-changing, non-solid world. Then we can feel confidence which has nothing to do with the illusion of certainty. We can feel held without holding on, without clogging the holes in knowledge through which we leak and disperse throughout space, disintegrating into particles, into parts of particles and the spaces between them, those that constitute the individual phenomenon, whose subjective perspective produces the illusion of a self. If we develop F in O, we will be able to bear reality and be in touch with it. If we develop *saddhā*, we will be able to feel safety and solace which do not have illusion as their base. If we develop an open-eyed trust, a non-false trust whose object is the truth, then we can feel embraced by the arms of an unstable universe that keeps changing, a universe whose origin – for us at least – is an explosion that set off a motion of dispersal, which has only been accelerating ever since.

Notes

1 In the environment-individual setup (Winnicott, 1975a, p. 99).
2 The assumption regarding the existence of a "true self" chimes with one of our most fundamental intuitions, as well as with ancient Eastern philosophies – those that developed into present-day Hinduism, and their attitude to "atman" – an essential self-core, immutable and independent. In this approach, *atman* (the self) is *brahman* (the power or principle behind absolute reality, the essence of everything; Biderman, 1995). Thus, once you have touched and found within yourself the immaterial heart of things, the essence of essences, the thing that cannot be further divided, that cannot be described, that cannot be perceived – then you have found the truth, eternity, god, the power that rules everything (the ancient texts that describe these ideas are the Upanishads). The Buddha subverted this view. He showed that thorough analysis leads to awareness of "anatman" (Pāli: *anattā*) – the absence of selfhood – as one of the three features of existence. All phenomena are "not-self", lack independent selfhood, are conditioned and time-bound, and can be broken down.
3 *Saṃvaṭṭati* and *vivaṭṭati*. Here *saṃvaṭṭati* means "dissolves" and *vivaṭṭati* means "evolves" (Bhikkhu Bodhi, 2010, note 6); that is, the first means "destruction" and the second, "renewal". But according to Rhys Davids and Stede (1921–1925, p. 637), the meaning of *saṃvaṭṭati* is actually "involve", and *vivaṭṭati*'s original meaning is "devolve", also used to denote the absence of *vaṭṭa* (which is the same as the absence of *saṃvaṭṭa*), i.e., *nibbāna* or liberation from *saṃsāra*.
4 The ruling faculties: *indriya*; the overpowering forces: *bala*.
5 *pakati saddhā*
6 *bhāvanā saddhā*
7 *ānāpāna sati*
8 For some of these factors, see the section "Subtle pleasantness" in Chapter 3.
9 The selected fact is a certain fact that suddenly comes to the psychoanalyst's mind and casts a new light on details that seemed unrelated or unreasonable. As a result, hitherto fragmentary material appears coherent and meaningful (Bion, 1962b, pp. 72–74. Inspired by H. Poincaré).
10 *Tisaraṇaṃ Gamanaṃ*

References

Barnea-Astrog, M. (2017). *Hitbaharut: Vipassana, Psychoanalysis, and the Mind Investigating Itself* [Hebrew]. Tel Aviv: Resling

Berman, E. (2009). Introduction to "Ego distortion in terms of true and false self". In: D. W. Winnicott, *True Self, False Self: Essays, 1935–1963*, edited by E. Berman (pp. 199–201). Tel Aviv: Am Oved.

Bhikkhu Bodhi (2010). A translation of Brahmajāla Sutta: The All-embracing Net of Views (DN 1). *Access to Insight*. Accessed June 27, 2018 at: www. accesstoinsight.org/tipitaka/dn/dn.01.0.bodh.html.

Biderman, S. (1995). *Early Buddhism*. Tel Aviv: The Ministry of Defence.

Bion, W. R. (1957). Differentiation of the psychotic from the non-psychotic personalities. *International Journal of Psycho-Analysis, 38*: 266–275.

Bion, W. R. (1959). Attacks on linking. *International Journal of Psycho-Analysis, 40*: 308–315.

Bion, W. R. (1962). *Learning from Experience*. London: Tavistock.

Bion, W. R. (1963). *Elements of Psycho-Analysis*. London: Heinemann.

Bion, W. R. (1970). *Attention and Interpretation*. London: Tavistock.

DN 27.

Eigen, M. (1985). Toward Bion's starting point: between catastrophe and faith. *International Journal of Psycho-Analysis, 66*: 321–330.

Eigen, M. (2004). *Psychic Deadness*. London: Karnac.

Fleischman, P. R. (2013). *Wonder: When and Why the World Appears Radiant*. Amherst: Small Batch Books.

Gampel, Y. (2004). Introduction to: Wilfred R. Bion, *Learning from Experience*. Tel Aviv: Bookworm.

Goenka, S. N. (2004). *The Discourse Summaries: Talks from a Ten-Day Course in Vipassana Meditation* (condensed by William Hart). Igatpuri, India: Vipassana Research Institute.

Ledi Sayadaw (2009). *The Manuals of Dhamma*. U Nyana Sayadaw, Baruna Beni, U Sein Nyo Tun & U Saw Tun Teik (Trans.). Igatpuri: Vipassana Research Institute.

Matri, Y. (2005). *Psyche's Home*. Ben-Shemen: Modan.

Nathanson, D. L. (1986). The empathic wall and the ecology of affect. *Psychoanalytic Study of the Child, 41*: 171–186.

Nothnagel, K. (2015). A translation of Dhajaggasutta (SN 11.3), lesson 1.4.3, verses for protection. *Exploring the path, online Pāli program*. Accessed June 16, 2018 at: learning.pariyatti.org/mod/page/view.php?id=223.

Nyanatiloka (1997). *Buddhist Dictionary: Manual of Buddhist Terms and Doctrines* (4th revised edn). Nyanaponika (Ed.). Kandy, Sri Lanka: Buddhist Publication Society.

Pelled, E. (2005). *Psychoanalysis and Buddhism: On the Human Capacity to Know*. Tel Aviv: Resling.

Rhys Davids, T. W., & Stede, W. (Eds.) (1921–1925). *The Pāli Text Society's Pāli–English Dictionary*. Chipstead: Pāli Text Society.

SN 11.3.

SN 12.15.

SN 12.23.

U Ko Lay (Trans.) (2005). Aggañña Sutta. In: *Suttanta Piṭaka, Dīgha Nikāya: Collection of Numerically Graduated Discourses. A Translation of Pāthika Vagga Pāḷi.* Edited by The Editorial Committee, Department for the Promotion and Propagation of the Sāsanā. U Tum Mya Aung: Yangon.

Winnicott, D. W. (1975). Anxiety associated with insecurity. In: *Through Paediatrics to Psycho-Analysis* (pp. 97–100). London: Hogarth & the Institute of Psycho-Analysis.

Winnicott, D. W. (2016). Ego distortion in terms of true and false Self. In: L. Caldwell & H. Taylor Robinson (Ed.). *The Collected Works of D. W. Winnicott: Volume 6, 1960–1963* (pp. 159–174). New York: Oxford University.

Chapter 5

Attention as an environment

From our moments of wonder, let there be a harvest of realism and reverence

– Fleischman, 2013, p. 352

Gentleness may appear in the company of fragility on the one hand and of destructiveness on the other. For the gentle person, one of life's missions is to disentangle the knot into which these forces are tied and to know her gentleness: to tell it apart from fragility, to set both free from destructiveness, and to find gentleness a place where it can be tenderly held while it serves as a basis for growth. For this to occur, prolonged exposure to truth, open-eyed faith, and devotion are required, but also the right kind of response from the environment.

The environment consists of material and mental aspects, and the latter include elements experienced as internal and elements experienced as external. In the next pages I consider attention as an environment: the ways in which its qualities constitute an intrapersonal and an interpersonal space, with particular features that either support or don't support gentleness, that either support or don't support processes of healing and growth.

Conditioned arising: self–environment relations

Our environment is our zone of living. We breathe it, we eat it, we absorb it, we take it in. We breathe into it, empty ourselves into it, seep into it, resonate with it. The environment takes part in our becoming, and we participate in its creation. Psychoanalysis describes these processes in terms of the dynamics between introjection and projection. The Pāli canon tells us that we are sustained by material nutriment and by immaterial nutriment. The material nutriment is what we consume in the form of food and drink. The immaterial nutriment is of three kinds: contact with our surroundings, that is, the impressions left on us by our incessant encounter with objects from all sense spheres; the accumulated residues formed by past reactions, which, along with the current sensory input, feed our stream of consciousness; and this stream of consciousness, from which the reactions in the present moment arise. In one fascinating discourse, "the discourse on the knowledge of the beginning" (DN 27), the Buddha tells how material, once ingested, slowly changes the body's physical characteristics, how these physical characteristics affect the mental activity of the owner of this body, and how this mental activity, in its turn, leads to changes not only in this creature but also to changes in the environment and in the food it produces, which goes on changing the body's characteristics as it is ingested, and so on. Our food, whether material or immaterial, is important; and between inside and outside, between matter and mind, there is a constant process of exchange.

Let us think, for example, about some of the building blocks of the self. Let us consider the memories, which the self conceives as its property (Bion, 1970), those that play such a significant role in creating the self's experience as an essential phenomenon with an enduring core. After all, those recollections, those ostensibly solid possessions, fixed in time it would seem, this luggage that the psyche carries along in spite of its ongoing transformations, in spite of the ongoing transformations of the body and of life's circumstances – they are not really that stable and unchanging. It would therefore be interesting, in this context, to probe the process set off by memory's non-solidity in its encounter with the world.

Recent research has been discussing the *re-consolidation* of memories, a process whereby a memory, whenever it comes to mind, temporarily enters a state of instability, a state of plasticity in which it can be updated and reconstituted (Besnard, Caboche, & Laroache, 2012). Like everything else in the mind, memory is neither solid nor static: it is "a dynamic process undergoing continual reorganization as a function of the ongoing experience of the organism" (Przybyslawski & Sara, 1997). The original memory – if one wishes to refer to it as such – was created in the past; but, remaining active, its impact on the present continues. Recollection is a present event in every sense of the word, and a present event is always open to change. And so memory is not some autonomous possession but a time-dependent constructive process which goes on taking in and assimilating new information (Hupbach et al., 2007).

Memories are traces left in the mind by past experiences. They consist of the complex of sense impressions received and perceived by the mind, the sensations it experienced, and the reactions these triggered. From a Buddhist perspective, the mental luggage involved in memories can be taken as "*kammic* residues": patterns of attitude and reaction (*saṅkhāra*)[1] linked to patterns of perception (*saññā*)[2] and sensation which emerged in the mind in the course of its history of experiences. Experiences that evoked powerful and prolonged reactions get deeply engraved. Experiences that trigger feeble reactions register as light touches. Experiences may be pleasurable, traumatic, or casual, and reactions may be conscious or unconscious. Either way, when the present circumstances awaken residues left behind by past events, they surface in the form of present experiences.

A present experience is an active experience, and an active experience is one that is being shaped depending on the encountered conditions. An important element of these conditions (the most important, it seems to me) consists of the qualities of the internal and external environment of attention. A residue associated with an experience of danger which is resurrected in circumstances marked by a sense of safety will assimilate some of the qualities of this safety, then to return to the mind having been affected by them, at least somewhat. A residue associated with a bad sense of self, shame that evolved from ongoing exposure to contempt or criticism, and arises in an inter-psychic domain characterized by love and acceptance will absorb some of this love and acceptance and change as a result, no matter how minute the change and even though it may, for the time being, remain concealed. This is especially the case when the process is attended by awareness of the experience. Then the safety, acceptance, and love that accompany the moment of recollection are bound to be more significantly absorbed by the system and to gradually change the way experience is organized and, as a result, change the concomitant behaviors and habitual patterns.

Change of this kind is change for the better: the system, in a state of plasticity, was presented with new and good conditions, and this led to the undoing of some of the existent disarray. This is one of the main aspects of the inter-psychic attentional environment as a healing element, and the ability to benefit from it depends on the features of the internal attentional environment – on the ability of the one who wants to be healed to be aware and not excessively reactive, to digest, internalize, and integrate. (It is in the nature of things that a mental organization which powerfully refuses reality, whether through massive projection or by other means, will also refuse the healing potential of the good environment.) Similarly, if the residue that registered during an experience of danger is awakened to encounter a sense of additional danger or persecution, it will reconsolidate itself in the mind once it has taken them in and will become engraved more deeply or in a more complicated manner. If the residue of shame arises in conditions of re-exposure to contempt or criticism, it is likely to absorb some of these and to go back to operate in the mind in an even more deeply entrenched way.

When working with the depths of the mind, whether through therapy or through meditation, one of the major processes is the one in which residues of the past arise in the present. These residues awaken as a result of certain present circumstances that remind the mind-body of similar circumstances it encountered in the past. Their resurrection activates the system in ways that reproduce, more or less, its earlier responses to those similar circumstances. What will determine, here, whether work is damaging or favorable is the attentional attitude that these materials, once aroused, meet: a blind reactive attitude will fuel the materials of suffering and solidify them; a balanced and heedful approach will digest them and eventually cause them to dissolve (Barnea-Astrog, 2017).

Fundamentally, therefore, the reactions of the mind itself are responsible for the reformation of the resurrected mental residues – they are the formative factors. But they entertain relations of dependency with the other present circumstances: physical and mental, external and internal. The event in which features of the environment touch the mind is mental nutriment as well. Danger and persecution, contempt and criticism, love, acceptance, and safety – they are all potential features of the internal environment; equally, they are conditions proffered objectively by the external environment, simply and truly, and which the mind either takes in or neutralizes – either to its advantage or not.

If we further increase the resolution of our examination, we will find that the process I describe here does not only obtain for the complexes considered significant in therapeutic work, not only for these knotty, thick, and heavy mental residues whose reawakening is so prominent in therapeutic dynamics and in life's more dramatic events. We will find that at every single moment, some traces of the past surface as a result of the present conditions that accord with them, and that due to their arising in the present, they become exposed to modification.

Every memory and its associated charge, every psycho-physical complex resulting from the mind's reaction to experience, undergoes change whenever it arises. It takes in some molecules of the present and perhaps releases some molecules of the past, then to return to the mind, where it dwells and operates in its new shape. When all past molecules of a memory have been dismantled – when, that is to say, the reactive charge it carried has been entirely neutralized (as a result of sufficient exposure to conditions of non-reaction and clear-eyed vision) – then it is eliminated as a suffering-producing *kammic* residue. It stops being an active and activating factor, and the mind is relieved of it. And to the extent that the mind is relieved of it and its likes – it is free.

If this is how things are, then we should do our best to create favorable present conditions. As therapists, teachers, or parents, we should seek to create a positive external attentional environment that will support the development of a positive internal attentional environment of our patients, students, or children. As meditators, as investigators of the mind, as thinking people, we should strive to cultivate our internal attentional environment: to sharpen and refine it and make it more spacious, to rid it of destructiveness and fill it with awareness, equanimity, and love. Naturally, it will flow out and also constitute a good external environment for those with whom we interact.

Associating: examining the elements around us

> Said Ānanda: "This is half of the holy life, having virtuous people as friends, companions and colleagues." "Don't say that, Ānanda", the Buddha replied. "Don't say that. Having virtuous people as friends, companions and colleagues is the whole of the holy life".
> –(Based on SN 45.2. In: Nothnagel, 2015)[3]

When asked by a congregation of lay disciples, "householders" like us, "What is the highest welfare?" the Buddha begins with the environment, human and non-human: avoidance of fools, the company of the wise – this is the highest welfare, he says. Living in a suitable environment, one that supports morality and the development of positive mental qualities – this is the highest welfare (Snp 2.4. Also in Goenka, 2006). Of course, one's surroundings are not everything, and so he continues: right aspirations for oneself, extensive education and skill, well-disciplined conduct, a soft, truthful way of talking – this is the highest welfare. Caring for one's relatives and serving them, a peaceful occupation – this is the highest welfare. Generosity, a virtuous, honest way of life, flawless deeds; disliking evil and keeping away from it, abstaining from intoxicating substances – this is the highest welfare. Respectfulness, gentleness, and modesty, contentment and gratitude;

patience and tolerance, willingness to receive guidance – this is the highest welfare. Listening to the Buddha's teachings and discussing them at the proper time; vigilant, ardent practice of the path; realizing the four noble truths; experiencing *nibbāna* – this is the highest welfare. When the mind, faced with the vicissitudes of life, remains unshaken, sorrowless, stainless, and secure; when one becomes invincible, safe and happy everywhere – this is the highest welfare (Snp 2.4. Also in Goenka, 2006).[4]

From the gross to the subtle, from the behavioral to the mental, from the external to the internal – this is how he explains. But first comes the environment: One who lives in a place that encourages dark thinking and unethical behavior is likely to be affected by this. One who lives in a place that encourages clear thinking and the development of universal moral virtues is likely to be affected by this. One who lives where there is an opportunity to be exposed to the four noble truths might well be exposed to them. One who lives in the company of those who follow the way leading from suffering to happiness is bound to receive support from them and guidance on her own way.

A good external environment, a growth-supportive environment, an environment that is a haven of truth – though it is not always an easy and comfortable place – depends first and foremost on a mind that perceives it as such or that treats it in ways that will make it so; yet it also relies on the features of the external surroundings themselves. Not every environment is favorable, supportive of growth, a home. And the clearer the mind, the better able it is at pinpointing this. Whenever it is possible, it prefers to be in a positive environment; it copes in a more balanced manner when it has no choice but to be in a not-so-healthy ambience for a while. At the highest levels of liberation, clearly, a person is set free of any mental dependence on his setting: whether it is positive or negative, pleasant or unpleasant, adjusted or unadjusted – it can no longer hurt him. He remains connected to his environment, entirely open – but it does not possess the power to upset his mental balance or to cause him misery: this is because his internal climate is fully developed and ridded of any defilement. Those who follow the path leading to this non-dependence and are yet far from having become immune to mental suffering must consider their surroundings and ensure that they are as nourishing as possible. Not due to the elemental pull to avoid pain and to wallow in pleasure: pleasure is not necessarily good, nor is pain necessarily bad. Rather, as the Buddha proposed, those who follow the path should seek conditions that will support them in the process of liberation from suffering and illusion.

A sense of environmental toxicity

Many sensitive people live with a feeling that reality itself penetrates them. This sense of penetrability is unpleasant; it is associated with lack of protection and it arouses anxiety. For Grotstein (1995), the source of all anxiety, unlike realistic fear, is projective identification. We can add that the anxiety entailed by projective identification is related to an experience of being penetrated by a toxic environment. An experience is an experience, and it depends on the way in which the subjective apparatus receives, perceives, and produces it. Toxicity is an experience as well, but often, the experience originates from objective characteristics, actual violent features of the setting.

So let us distinguish three factors: the toxic features of the environment as such; the subject's sensitivity to these features, that is to say, the degree to which she does or does not sense them; and her vulnerability in the face of these, which is the extent to which she is hurt by them in proportion to the extent to which she is capable of being protected from them, i.e., of being able to neutralize their toxic effect on her. In this context, the environmental features are determined by the degree of ignorance, greed, and hatred present and their specific manifestations. The subject's sensitivity is related to the level of her conscious-perceptual-sensory resolution. Her vulnerability is associated with the relations between the reactive strata of her mind and her ability to be in touch with reality, see it clearly, and remain firm in the face of it, even when it is difficult.

And thus, from time to time the interpersonal sphere is bound to be charged with envy, greed, contempt, loathing, alienation, and imperviousness, with explicit or concealed forms of aggression. A person who is not particularly sensitive will hardly perceive these mental materials, and unless they become really excessive and express themselves in blunt verbal or physical actions, she will dismiss them. Another, more sensitive person will experience these things with every fiber of his being. They will chafe his unhealed wounds and ache him; as a result, his reality perception will be distorted, inducing him to react in ways that will further injure him. A third person, also very sensitive, will experience these mental substances very vividly. But her mind, having already been somewhat cleared, and with some of its coarsest luggage removed, will be better at perceiving the chain of events. She will be less reactive to them and will therefore suffer less. In this way she may also contribute towards a clarification of the situation for the others, if only by not worsening it.

Discord and harmony

The mind that manifested a high degree of sensitivity towards the toxicity of its surroundings is likely to show a similar sensitivity towards other aspects of it and towards the degree of compatibility or incompatibility it seems to have with it. Compatibility and incompatibility can be addressed in aesthetic terms like those of discord and harmony.

Gentleness involves a sense of aesthetics. Gentle children may hear music in the sound of water flowing from the tap, in the play of the wind, the rumbling of the fridge. They may see orderly shapes in leaves on the ground, the food on their plate, everyday objects casually put on a shelf. If life does not force them to clench their jaws and become impervious, they will continue being sensitive to beauty and its absence in adulthood. The aesthetic sensibility will of course occur in many formations, and it doesn't necessarily express itself exclusively in what is commonly perceived as artistic modes. It might appear in the form of a gift for mathematics or in a love of nature, a drive for the truth or a sense of humor that captures subtleties. In a gentle person this comes together with ethical sensitivity, which is another expression of the beautiful, the concordant, the upright. In any case, the aesthetic sensibility creates a yearning for harmony and a sensitivity to whatever jars. The gentle person, to be happy, must learn to identify the sense of discord whenever it arises in him, to accept his sensitivity to this, to direct himself to harmonious action and to develop his ability to tolerate situations in which the absence of consonance is inevitable.

Discord and harmony; right adjustment and tuning – ancient cultures used musical concepts to describe ethical qualities. Discordant sounds, musical disharmony, and ill-tuned musical instruments have been used as metaphors for evil; agreeable combinations of sounds and well-tuned instruments have represented goodness (Thanissaro Bhikkhu, 2006). One familiar discourse of the Buddha refers to Sona the monk. Sona overstrained himself in his meditation practice and, not getting the spiritual results he was aiming for, he thought he might as well give it all up and return to ordinary family life. The Buddha saw this, appeared before him, and instructed him otherwise: to adjust his effort as one adjusts the strings of a lute. The effort, he explained to Sona, like a string, must be sufficiently tightened: neither too loose nor too taut. Both when it is too loose and when it is too taut, the string will fail to produce the wished-for sound. The middle path is required here: the path between laziness – causing the meditator to abandon his practice – and excess effort leading to tension, agitation, and restlessness, which in their turn might similarly

lead the meditator to quit (AN 6.55). The quality of the meditator, therefore, is the quality of attunement. This refers to the measure of effort,
but not only that: the truly spiritual person is always in tune with what's
good and right (Thanissaro Bhikkhu, 2006).

We can see that recognizing toxic elements – whether internal or
external – is a specific instance of perceiving disharmony. We can add
that where conditions allow, it is possible to use the sense of discord-
ance to identify harmful or unfitting elements, and that we might relate
to the sense of harmony as a sign of the presence of nourishing elements
and of accord. In this context we may distinguish between two levels
of discord and harmony: the universal level and the personal-local. On
the universal level, discord relates to the domain the Buddha defined
as *akusala*: the domain of impure, damaging actions whose fruits are
shackles and distress. Simply put, we can identify the elements belong-
ing in this domain when, in examining them, we find that they are
derivatives of the three roots of evil: ignorance, craving, and hate. All
the other destructive factors, some of which have been mentioned in
earlier chapters, are also included in the domain of the harmful – as
specific instances of these three roots or extensions or manifestations
of them. On the local level, by contrast, discord refers to a certain
context-dependent incompatibility. One woman, for instance, will be
happy to live in the big city, while another will feel overwhelmed and
suffocated. For one person, so-and-so will be the perfect partner – for
another, insufferable. Taking up the study of law, or finding a job in a
psychiatric hospital, or getting early retirement, or having a child, or
giving up on having a family, or adopting a dog, or participating in a
detox workshop – these might be just the right thing at the right time
for one person, while for another person – or for the same one in different circumstances – they may be a recipe for misery. Still, because
the universal and the personal mix into each other, the two levels of
harmony and discord are also not separate. If it is to lead to happiness,
personal compatibility must be situated in the field of *kusala* – the field
of universal good. So, when someone finds herself attracted to an environment dominated by imperviousness and exploitation and it seems to
her that she is in the right place, what she feels is not a compatibility
based on harmony but rather the result of the lines stretching between
her internal violence and the external violence that surrounds her. Similarly, one who gets outraged by certain characteristics of the people or
situations she encounters might not necessarily be responding to their
actual features. It may very well be that the sense of discord she feels is
the product of her own reactive strata.

When is it, then, that the mind identifies disharmony? And when can we trust this identification? I formulate it as follows: As long as the mind tends to act violently towards experience, the feelings of toxicity and discord arising in it will often be reflections of reality-distortions, products of the heart's anguish which through acts of splitting and projection is looking in vain for a way out. Reality, it seems to this mind, is aggressive, evil, toxic. It seems this way because as it touches the mind, it awakens its internal frictions, and this is painful. As the mind develops, however, it rids itself of its self-destructiveness and fragility, and its feelings reflect reality's actual characteristics more frequently. Wherever the accumulations of pain and ignorance still cause it to be clouded over, it will falter and stumble; usually, however, it will be able to tell the universally harmful from the nonharmful and the personally, particularly, locally compatible from the incompatible. It will be able to take heed of the voices that instruct it to keep away, as much as possible, from the universally damaging and from the locally incompatible, and it will be able to take in those elements that harmonize with what's good and right inside it, with what's good and right in the world.

Two species of accuracy

One who walks the path of gentleness seeks to adjust himself to a certain tone, the tone of truth. When he is in tune with the beautiful and the good, he feels in harmony; he feels good. When he strays from the path, he feels discord and understands reparation is due. Like a musician, he listens carefully; he is attentive to the internal and to the external, to the encounter between them, to their interrelations and their relations with the proper sound. Such attention requires a considerable degree of accuracy: an accuracy linked to awareness of the body and its sensations, to the mind and its contents; an accuracy that enables him to pick up on subtleties.

When we consider accuracy, it's worth making the distinction between accuracy as such, which has the properties I have just described, and anxious accuracy, which is associated with suffering. This latter species of accuracy is reflected in a need to attach realization to the idea. To attach: to tighten the membrane, to firmly hold a spatula and spread (realization) carefully (over the idea). In this sense, striving for accuracy is associated with the dread of non-existence and with second-skin mechanisms. If the mind carries a conception and is unable to bear the gap between it and reality, then it will try to force reality into adhering to the conception, come what may. (The opposite, it seems to me, is not true in this case. The attempt to change the conception so it will make a better fit with reality belongs in a slightly different domain of mental activity, I believe.) If it fails to bring them close enough together, the psyche imagines, it will leak through the cracks and scatter. Trying to keep realization glued to the conception demands a great effort. The psyche's strings are clearly overstretched and hence, in the Buddha's terms, there is no chance they will produce the right sound.

The other type of accuracy occurs in realistic terms of discord and harmony, and it is attended by mental equanimity. Equanimity sharpens the mind and makes it precise. The sharpened mind discerns reality's characteristics – impermanence, discontent, lack of selfhood – and recognition of these leads to deeper equilibrium. The mind, in this case, is taut and loose in the right proportions. It attends to both the inner and outer reality, and like one with perfect pitch, it seeks maximum calibration and tuning. The utilitarian self, greedy and anxious, is not part of this process. Here, realization is *sammā*-realization, conception is *sammā*-conception. This is a type of accuracy which doesn't cling.

Inner attentional environment: the mental space

In spite of the beauty of gentleness, expressed in sensitivity and the aspiration for harmony, it cannot host true prosperity unless the ability to bear disharmony occurs along with it. This requires a mental space capable of tolerating frustration, a mental space Bion discusses at length.

The ability to tolerate frustration, according to Bion, is needed to learn from experience and to be in touch with ultimate reality (O). In this sense, *khanti pāramī*, patience and forbearance, is crucial in the exploration of the unknown which is entailed by the act of faith. For Bion the mental space is unknowable, a thing-in-itself that can be represented by means of thoughts (Bion, 1970). Thought is by definition frustrating as it approaches experience but doesn't fully grasp or embody it. This is why thought may be insufferable for those who find it hard to tolerate frustration. Those whose ability to tolerate frustration is better developed may also experience something similar when they try to employ thought in order to touch preverbal materials, materials with which they don't have enough experience to identify a constant conjunction, to know and represent them. In such a case, thought constrains on the one hand, but on the other it also releases intuition, and there is conflict between the drive to leave the intuition unexpressed and the wish to express it. Those who can bear the inherent limitation on representation will have the ability to connect with their preverbal materials.[5] Those who cannot bear this will be unable to make this contact and will miss out on the relief thought can bring (Bion, 1970).

The relief of thoughts. What is the nature of this relief? What characterizes these thoughts? Relief may be superficial – substituting pleasure for tension by using its objects as objects of desire. Thought that achieves this kind of relief is largely hallucinatory; that is, it intentionally produces mental objects that arouse pleasant sensations with the aim of masking unpleasant sensations from which the mind recoils. Another common type of thinking activity that occurs in the field that is subject to the pleasure principle involves removing oneself from internal reality by means of the systematic filling of gaps in knowing. This covering up of gaps soothes anxiety on the one hand, and on the other constitutes a source of gratification provided by a false sense of knowing and control. Here, thought acts to block out revelation: the person already knows what happened and why (Eigen, 2004), and his field of investigation is foreclosed. He might be doing this because he "cannot take the build-up of tension involved in the growth of a thought or feeling" (Eigen, 2004, Kindle location 1395). He might be doing this because he "learned from bitter experience that emotional reality is worthless or impossible" (ibid.). If that's how it operates, thinking leads to "hardening psychic arteries" (Eigen, 2004, Kindle location 1307).

But thoughts might, by contrast, be a means (or a product or an expression) of digesting reality by the mind's digestive system. When this is the case, thoughts involve contact with certain layers of the truth. The more thoughts arise as a result of dwelling on the present experience in a non-saturated state of mind – one in which the mind is free, temporarily at least, of craving for experience, or resistance to it, or of covering it up with imaginary creations; of distraction and of attachment to the soothing sensation of false knowledge – the closer they approach deeper layers of truth. Relief, in this case, is the result of a real transformation in the mind's materials. It is the result of emerging – to some degree or another – from some entanglement; of being set free – to some degree or another – from some shackle. It is the result of clarification.

Clear thought is both an outcome of and a contributor to finding one's way in mental space. It is a manifestation of developing the mental equipment necessary for understanding the processes of inner reality. It becomes possible when the mind's equipment evolves to the extent that it can distinguish thought taking place in the domain of the pleasure principle from thought that subverts it. Such equipment can tell the difference when thought aims to create pleasantness and to mask unpleasantness;

when it is motivated by anxiety and hatred, which cause a turning away from reality; when it leads to mental stasis and when, by contrast, to insight and growth.

The interpersonal attentional environment: quiet love and openness to truth

The interpersonal climate is the product of the communication between one internal climate and another. Winnicott (1971) referred to this communication, among other things, in terms of mirroring. A mirror is a lifeless, passive object, on the face of it; when neither stained nor malformed, it will reflect the person in front of it more or less faithfully. In the human domain, however, we do not face a mirror: what we have is two (or more) mind-body phenomena that interrelate, engage in elaborate exchanges on various channels, simultaneously or successively, openly or covertly. A mirror, when placed opposite another mirror, produces infinite reflections. When one limbic system[6] faces another, they will resonate with each other and affect one another continuously. Winnicott drew our attention to this:

> What does the baby see when he or she looks at the mother's face? I am suggesting that, ordinarily, what the baby sees is himself or herself. In other words the mother is looking at the baby and what she looks like is related to what she sees there. All this is too easily taken for granted. I am asking that this which is naturally done well by mothers who are caring for their babies shall not be taken for granted.
>
> (1971, p. 112)

The profound contribution of these simple sentences lies in the accuracy and clarity with which they capture the exchange of mental materials constituting the inter-psychic, dependent relations of becoming: the infant sees in the mother's face the mother who sees him. It is her state of mind as she sees him, the way she perceives him, feels him, and reacts to him, that determines the qualities displayed in her face; when the infant registers, perceives, and senses them, they largely institute the manner in which he perceives and senses himself.

A person is not merely the product of her parent's gaze. Not all of her traits, abilities, and limitations are entailed by early object relations, by successful holding and containment, by the sufficient or insufficient compatibility of her environment. But she is deeply influenced by them:

they entertain complex, enduring relations with her personal luggage, physical and mental, in which they take part. If she is very sensitive, she will experience these intensely, for better and for worse. If in her adult life she follows the way of gentleness, trying to sharpen her mind and gradually dissolve its residues of destructiveness, she will, for good reasons, seek an environment that looks at her with kind eyes.

Much like the parent, the therapist's most significant responsibility is to present the person assisted by her with a setting that naturally supports processes of discovery and growth. It is the therapist's attention that is largely responsible for this creation: If she can steadily take an attentional position combining Winnicott's holding, Balint's favorable, understanding environment, Kurtz's loving presence, and Bion's flexible and open container (with emphasis on links F and O, which are necessary non-linear conditions for conveying the profound, unconventional truth), then she will produce a good environment. This combination has the advantages of including a non-egocentric investment in the relationship, an intent for calibration and adjustment, and the willingness to encounter mental reality and to digest it even when it's hard, so as to get to the truth without which no growth is possible. I believe that the phrase "quiet love and openness to the truth" renders this very well, and as long as we stick to western psychodynamic thinking, it seems to offer the ideal living conditions for the mind – whether gentle or not. Such an environment offers the patient (or, better: the self-observing person) an opportunity to take in its beneficial elements. And, provided his internalizing abilities are functional and he doesn't suffer overly severe internal attacks on linking, in due time these beneficial elements become inextricable parts of his internal reality, of his self.

It is no coincidence that these qualities of therapeutic attention and the processes they facilitate derive from maternal-parental qualities. The latter are universal qualities and processes, and this makes them relevant and important a great deal beyond the clinical situation. Not every interpersonal situation calls for our use of all their aspects, and in many ways, this, indeed, isn't our responsibility. But if we take our thought one step further, we will see that, were it not for our limitations, we would strive to create both within and among us a similar climate, always, and in all circumstances. Every situation, obviously, requires its specific, appropriate attitude, but the mental foundation for this appropriate attitude is basically the same. The Buddha's way leads, among other things, to the development of four mental qualities, called *Brahma vihāra*: the sublime mental qualities that characterize Brahma, a supreme heavenly entity, or the states in which he abides or dwells. These four mental qualities are *mettā* – loving-kindness, a love shorn of desire or egoism; *karuṇā* – compassion; *muditā* – sympathetic joy, joy at the other's success and joy (complementing envy, on the one hand, and greed, on the other); and *upekkhā* – perfect mental equilibrium, the zero point between pain and pleasure, the non-preference for any one of them, and in the present context, also the non-preference for any creature over another, as all equally deserve *mettā, karuṇā*, and *muditā*. This is why these qualities are also known as the "boundless" states – they are unlimited both in quantity and in terms of to whom they are directed: they are unbiased, extended everywhere.

To some extent, every mental quality of the internal environment spills into the external environment. But the four *Brahma vihāra* (especially *mettā*, perhaps) are a priori meant to diffuse and touch others. One who has cleared her mind of ignorance, craving, and hatred, false perception and erroneous views, of doubt, laziness, restlessness, fear, and anxiety, and who developed, instead, penetrating wisdom and clear vision, infinite love, non-egocentric joy, boundless compassion, and perfect mental poise – has she not created the optimal attentional environment inside herself and around her? Is this not the ideal climate to live in, a climate that does no harm, that is only beneficial? No matter how far removed we are from such a condition (I can only speak for myself), we have to acknowledge this as the goal. And to be able to reach it, we have to identify it, understand the way leading to it, and without being deluded about ourselves, or alternatively, without beating ourselves up for what we are and what we are not, we must harness our effort and faith so as to start walking along it. Every day we scatter the materials of our ignorance and suffering around us, damaging the mental climate of others and our own. But we can also move in the opposite direction: a little less lust, a little less imperviousness, a little less aggression, a little less clinging to illusive knowledge; a little more attention suffused with non-craving love – and the space in which we live changes, shifting the conditions for those who are with us as well. The person who faces us sees in our face how we see her. Our mental qualities spring from our face, our voice, our very presence – and when she perceives and senses them as they are, they affect the way she experiences, at that moment, herself and the world.

Marina: to lend an ear to the feeble, to see the hidden through a veil

The path refines. It takes apart what seemed of one piece and dissolves the solid; it heightens sensuous and perceptual resolution and sharpens the ability to discern. The gentle infant needs fine-tuned maternal attention to be held, attention that is internalized in due time to transform into a holding internal environment. He needs a maternal or paternal container that is open and ready to take in his contents down to their finest points, a container which, one day, will be internalized to turn into a healthy mental digestive system of its own. One who walks on the path explained by the Buddha needs others who experience reality at a resolution at least as high as his or her own and a social-cultural-conceptual context that elucidates and acknowledges it, as well as a sensitive and balanced internal space in which the subject matter of reality can arise and subside without turning into new accumulations of suffering. In both cases, the combination between a well-developed internal space and a fitting external space yields a living environment that supports the possibility of being safely gentle.

Attention is this space or environment. What happens when an experience receives attention does not happen, or happens differently, when it does not receive attention. What happens when the attention turned to experience is judgmental is unlike when it is non-judgmental. What happens or may happen when attention is blunt or invasive is unlike what happens or may happen when it is sharp or spacious. Attention's presence, absence, and degree, as well as its qualities, make up the features of the mental setting in which certain processes may or may not happen, in a variety of ways, invited into the domain of emotional processing or pushed away from it.

To illustrate a subtle level of interpersonal work with an attentional environment, I present some of the major motifs of Marina's process. Marina is a developmental psychologist in her mid-forties. A gentle woman, without a doubt, and her gentleness is mature and strong. She is experienced in exploring her mind, highly conscious of the flow of her experience and maintaining close and frequent touch with it. Against this background of familiarity with mental life, the feebleness of her emotional sphere (which is, of course, one component of the flow of experience) stands out. When an emotion, especially a disturbing one, arises in her, she has to make an effort – to invest in a conscious, deliberate act – in order to connect with that emotion and to allow it expression so as to become a living presence.

What happens to her, systematically and habitually, is the following: The emotion appears as a slight impression and then immediately passes. If for some reason the dynamic between inside and outside causes it to grow stronger, self-regulation mechanisms rapidly come into action to attenuate and weaken it. The emotion's volume is so low that it's never clear whether there is even a point in looking at it. It presents itself as a mental component that requires no attention. What remains, for Marina, is a sense that everything is all right; that whatever comes up, whether faint or slightly more present, will anyway shortly fade.

The sense of calm derived from the realization that anything that arises is destined to pass is anchored in the wisdom of impermanence. So, we are really dealing with subtleties here, and a keen eye is necessary: an eye that distinguishes between this wisdom, which is true and realistic, and the mental adhesions joining it like stowaways, using it in order to pass unnoticed below the radar of awareness. This is always a danger, I find, in the case of those who turn to various psychological and spiritual theories, ideas, and practices, however positive: The mind tends to attach its bad habits to innocent structures and contents, to, as it were, give the former a stamp of approval, justify them, cleanse them of their dark origins. The harshest cases I can think of right now are associated with the impure products of some forms of religious or ideological devotion. Other examples are the hallowing of anguish and mental agitation mistakenly perceived as indispensable to a life of creativity and contemplation, or treating family life and livelihood as the ultimate value to cover up an avoidance of mental reality and existential questions. These adhesions are a lot more subtle for people who consistently investigate their mind (by means of various types of Buddhist meditation; by means of in-depth psychotherapy; by other realistic and moral means) – but here too they must be identified.

Of course, our ability to pick up on these stowaways, when disguised as wisdom and balance they infiltrate the domain identified as pure, is limited. Ignorance is ignorance, and it lies in its nature to camouflage itself and the way it operates. All-embracing ignorance blocks out reality in an all-embracing manner. Local ignorance, pockets of it, hides patches of reality. Condensed layers of crude ignorance cover whatever they cover with an impermeable or nearly impermeable overlay (though this doesn't mean it will be so forever). Thin, perforated layers of ignorance have the effect of a scarf or veil: they reveal a bit and conceal a bit more; they allow elements and processes to glimmer through, next to immediately make them disappear, elusive, hazy hints and flashes in the corner of the eye, on the tip of the tongue, I thought I saw a shadow, I turned my head and it was gone, I must have dreamed.

Such was Marina's habit. Her mental life, apparently, at the very beginning must have demanded a system that would guard against her emotions intensifying, the guiding reason being that as long as they did not overfill and cross a certain threshold – a particularly low one – they would not be accompanied by any need. In this way, understood Marina's mind, arranging itself accordingly, the need to take care of those feelings, and of herself as she was experiencing them, wouldn't arise. The need for someone to take care of her or those feelings would not arise. "Look – there's a feeling, now, perhaps pain, a yearning, a hint of distress – but it's so feeble it already passes, it takes care of itself. So, really, there's nothing for me to work on. I actually have no real need at all". I had to acknowledge Marina's mental climate and accept it for what it was. To embrace warmly the possibility that "this is probably all there is. That there simply isn't anything else, nothing more profound, somewhere deep down, nothing really significant and important that must be revealed". Any other approach would, understandably, have been felt as imposing, an expression of violence.

Marina's self-regulatory capabilities served her well. We both assumed they helped her survive and develop at the beginning of life, continuing as a great resource in her adulthood. When there was no other choice, they enabled her to hold herself. They turned her into one who needs less and is therefore less exposed. And so it was only logical that when an interpersonal dynamic stretched or deepened a little beyond what felt safe, in other words, if it threatened to raise her emotions to beyond where they were easy to deal with, she would draw back from the interaction. Finding herself in a group situation, she would almost automatically put on a thoughtful expression and retreat into her interior realms. In an eye-to-eye situation, she could be extremely attentive, present, and engaged, but here too, unless she was in the therapist's chair, chances were she would grow absent every now and then. Still, because her mind was blessed with other abilities and also because she had earlier successful experiences of mental processing and growth, this dissociation and absence, too, she was aware of.

The place to which Marina withdrew was a no-place. Awaiting her were no imaginary delights, no affliction and soul-wrenching doubt. It was more empty than full, more nothing than something. And the escapades there were done to regulate mental intensities but were also the expression of a companion-desire (or a mother-desire or a sister-desire) that went deeper: this was the wish to cease, to move no more, a wish for non-existence.

This nothingness offered her important solace, and her psyche wished for me and significant others to acknowledge and to cherish it, to allow for it and love her in the way it formed her. As with the feebleness of emotion, here too, my accepting attitude to her choice for absence was a crucial component of the process. Crucial – but certainly not sufficient. Acknowledging the survival mechanisms and supporting them is the first stage, but the process must continue and touch the harsh experiences that entailed these survival mechanisms, as well as the absent nourishing experiences – those which, had they been available, would in all probability have taken her to other forms of organizing. In the present context it seems that one of Marina's missing experiences was that of a maternal mind adequate to emotion's full force, that would permit it to arise and increase without the inhibitory presence of a forceful self-regulating system. A mind, attentive and flexible, open enough to fear, sadness, and hatred because its own *reverie* was good enough, able to properly digest them and restore them to the daughter in a reasonable state, sufficiently attenuated – so that she would not have to learn prematurely how to moderate her feelings; so that later in life she would not have to moderate her feelings prematurely, as they present themselves.

The way Marina acquired for conducting herself in the world of emotions and relationships faced us with a danger: the danger that we would restrict ourselves to legitimating her withdrawals and her general way of coping, that we would be tempted to forget that even though "everything was all right", and even though she was quite capable of holding and regulating herself, there was something yet she was longing for, something long since forgotten and dropped out of her world. Exactly because it was almost invisible, this danger was real. Even now, as I write these words and Marina's image is in my mind, it's hard to believe them. "Danger" and "longing" and "need" – they are too intense for her mental field. Waves of self-regulation immediately wash over them, obscuring and attenuating them, and they blur. At those moments I have to remind myself the many signs of danger, longing, and need that emerged and presented themselves and which we, in spite of everything, transformed into objects of investigation.

"We deal with the unknown, which does not make things easier for us by adjusting itself to our mind's weak perceptual ability. The things we deal with are so delicate and implicit that they are hardly perceptible, and yet they are very real, capable of destroying us almost unawares" (Aharoni & Bergstein, 2012, pp. 44–45, note 32).[7] The longing Marina displayed was first and foremost for not-being. But there was something else that peeped from behind it, something that did want to capture what-was-just-at-the-tip-of-the-tongue,   what-was-slipping-from-the-corner-of-the-eye. Something seeking contact with emotion, reaching out to sense and hold it, something that didn't want to slacken and withdraw knowing that, like all others before it, this emotion too would fade and pass even before having unfolded, grown strong and exceeded the limit of what could be easily handled alone.

For this concealed part I am available; to this I lend an attentive ear. I ride the subterranean streams of the process, ready to encounter it at its faintest showing, no matter what form it takes. I am an attentional environment for it, trying to be good enough for just that – for it and the other parts, the other layers, the other subterranean and surfacing streams. An environment that doesn't urge but in its own way signals that here, it is safe. Here, it is possible. To be gentle with the present and the absent, with the faint and the increasing, the stormy and the mellow.

Holding and letting go

A sensitive and safe attentional environment enables the body-mind to develop a self-holding ability, yet also, and exactly as a result, to relax this self-holding and in certain conditions let it go. An attentional environment which can take in the undigested materials and return them to their origins when they have become meaningful and bearable, makes it possible for what previously spread through the system as nameless dread, flooded the entire being with terrible pain, or made it numb to its own vitality, to transform into growth-enabling substance. In this manner, on the one hand, the flooding and "excess" sensitivity undergo regulation and settle, while on the other, dullness gives way to sensitivity, and what was almost invisible receives attention, the longing for which had already been forgotten.

In an earlier publication (Barnea-Astrog, 2015) I discussed the case of a student who was investigating his restlessness, one of whose main expressions was the almost incessant jitteriness of his mental motion. Then, I didn't mention him by name; let's call him Peter. This is how I described him as he examined the nature of this mental dynamic and eventually discovered that each movement "was directed at its [mental] object like an arm extended, ready to push".

> Once he followed these movements, one push after another, he felt as though the metaphorical arms of his mind were pressing themselves, time and again, against what appeared an internal membrane; and that they were thus marking it, constituting it and sensing its existence. He wanted to know what would happen if he momentarily stopped stretching out the arms of his mind to push against the inner lining of the membrane. When he briefly managed to do so, he felt as if he vanished, scattered into space and turning into nothing.
>
> (Barnea-Astrog, 2015. In: *Hebrew Psychology*. Electronic version, translated from Hebrew)

"A young baby experiences the loss of mother's attention as being dropped. Suddenly he is not held, suddenly he is falling through space, unprotected, terrified of never being caught again and rescued" (Symington, 1985, p. 482). It was probably this type of experience that accompanied Peter and settled in one of the most archaic layers of his psyche. It prompted him (along with other factors which we must not pretend to know) to evolve a habitual mental behavior, which constituted for him, from within, the holding membrane that felt missing from the outside.

The missing element of holding, for Peter, was an attentional environment with the appropriate qualities; now, at last, when the time was ripe, given the right internal and external conditions, this very element came his way. In this state of full awareness, supported by an experimental-explorative attitude, surrounded by two or three pairs of eyes that looked at him sensitively and inquisitively, gentle and alert – the internal restlessness subsided and he found himself able to sink into a state of deep and wakeful calm. The survival-oriented function of his mind, which normally would have to extend its "arms", again and again, to stretch the membrane-walls of the inner space, that had to be producing his self boundaries constantly, and then again and again to reconfirm them – this function could now let go. It is hard to convey how significant such letting go can be for one who has hardly ever experienced it. And it is the outcome of a well-adjusted encounter of the external attentional environment with the inner climate of the psyche to which the former is directed.

For one person, the right attentional environment reduces free-floating anxiety and transforms the mental climate into something that allows a reasonable life. For another – or for the same person, at another point in time – the proper attentional environment enables hitherto silenced and blunted materials to appear. In both cases it hones the necessary conditions for the process of investigation and for release from painful patterns. In the first, anxiety which was dispersing within the body-mind raw, insufferable, undigested, fragmenting and fragmented beta elements, is regulated and processed; what was drenched in terror, on the verge of devastation, threatened to be dropped and to endlessly fall, to leak out, scatter through space – is collected unto itself, grows connecting tissue, sufficiently heals. In the second case, anxiety which had to be regulated, which had to and managed to be silenced and disrupted, which had to be kept below a certain threshold so as to stay controlled – finds the climate around it has changed. Now that climate is ready for it, requires no holding back, and instead allows it to express itself freely, spilling over, almost unbearable. It awakens and gets to be thought; and from a dismantling element, it slowly becomes one that joins. This connecting substance, though its origins are catastrophic, comes with its own effects: it clears away whatever it clears away and makes redundant whatever it makes redundant. In time, that which learned to hold itself in check now starts softening the connecting tissue. It releases muscles of body and mind which until now were effortfully clinched and leans back, allowing itself gaps through which it may leak, spill out to return soaked in reality. The mind trusts itself enough, trusts the universe, trusts itself within the universe and the universe within itself. This is not to say that anxiety has immediately grown less intolerable, less dreadful. The climate in which it arises, however, has changed. The attentional environment through which it flows has developed a different quality, and this quality metabolizes (and perhaps consumes), transmutes (and perhaps annihilates) the factors of suffering.

Here we have the dynamic between fragmentation and re-connection, between holding and non-clinging. In the right climate the mind has the freedom to hold itself and solidify, but also to let go, to dissolve and allow reality to pass through unimpeded. If, as was the case with both Marina and Peter, the person comes to therapy already equipped with an inner attentional environment supportive of growth, then the process evolves likes a blessing. Not rapid, necessarily, not fluent, perhaps, at times being difficult, making a clangor and a fuss, but proportionally illumined and mysterious, clear and intriguing enough for both of us to feel a profound sense of partnership. If, as in other cases, the inner attentional environment is relatively impoverished or too densely packed, more violent towards experience – then our shared life will be hard, full of adversity, anxiety, and distress. And yet it may very well be successful, provided we are (at least on some level) sufficiently patient and able, and willing enough to cooperate. For this to happen, we must both move with the mental reality as it presents itself and ride the waves of experience as best we can.

Non-clinging and movement

We have seen that for the meditator's attention to be moving systematically and in orderly fashion without getting stuck or becoming diffuse, she must be able to let go, and this requires a minimal degree of faith. (Of course this doesn't presuppose that faith and the ability to let go are already developed in her; they evolve as part of the process and develop her meditation in turn.) The same goes for the therapist: she needs faith to take her hands off (the clinging hands of her own resistance and desire) and yield to the movement – the movement occurring in the other in her presence, which instigates further movement: between her and him and within her. The therapist is a natural phenomenon, the person facing her is a natural phenomenon, and natural phenomena are in motion, always.

Movement is the outcome or expression of change, of the process of arising and fading away. Movement points at the three marks of existence. That whose nature it is to change – moves. If we wish to investigate the field of mind and matter, we must be able to follow movement.

One important reason why we need faith and the ability to let go is that free movement implies renunciation: renunciation of what is in the way of the movement. This can be incomplete, momentary, a renunciation which is an exercise in renunciation. But it must happen if the observant person wishes to follow with his attention the constant alteration of experience. What are the factors that allow him to do so, and what gets in his way? Generally speaking, these agree with the categories of beneficial and non-beneficial mental qualities which I presented above. More particularly, there are some aspects of the attentional attitude that are worth mentioning here. I don't claim to be exhaustive in my mapping, but below are some of these aspects.

Instrumental vs. non-instrumental thinking

Every active mental event is directed by a mental intention. A mental intention is an action (that is, *kamma*), and it refers to the mind's movement in a certain direction. The mental movement may be towards an experience, and it may be aiming away from it. Alternatively it might be marked by an attempt to inactivate itself in the face of this experience and not to move at all in its presence. Its specific qualities may take shape from envy, or greed, or disgust, or confusion, or cruelty, or despair, or self-sacrifice, or shame; from kind-heartedness, and gratitude, and the wish to serve the other, and modesty, and curiosity, and love, and compassion. In any case, according to the Buddha's teachings, it is the mental movement or intention that determines the outcome of the action: what our mind makes of its objects is what will – that instant and in time – "make" it.

One concealed expression of the movement "towards" or "away from" is instrumental thinking: the utilitarian approach to reality. We might consider ourselves extremely sensitive, conscious and compassionate, prosocial, process-oriented creatures – but we usually take this attitude to what we encounter, whether it be inside us or outside. On coming into contact with some mental component – a sensation, emotion, or any other mental subject matter – immediately, without being aware of it, we look for what we might do with or to it, how we might use it for our personal benefit; how we might, whether by taking it on or expelling it, avail ourselves of more pleasure and less pain. For the therapist too this is a default option into which the psyche flows easily and naturally, in the absence of any other clear conduit. The question "How may I help?" can give rise to wonderful mental, verbal, and physical actions, but it can just as easily fuel an attitude that strives to mold the materials of reality to fit a desirable image of the world and the correlated desirable sensations. No matter how subtle, such an approach is always founded on craving and anxiety. Craving and anxiety give birth to a pursuing type of attention, a searching one that "meets the sense-impressions half way, instead of awaiting their appearance" (Freud, 1911, p. 220), that seeks to take hold of reality components that one may or should, so it seems, manipulate. A mind bound up in the effort to chase and mold is a constrained mind that misses many details and layers of reality. Something will always be happening outside its purview – around it, behind it, above, below; something which quite often tends to be eye-opening and important.

Accordingly, both psychoanalytic listening and meditative attention aim at a non-selective, non-judgmental attentional approach. In seeking for such a quality of attention, we must make a separation between it and a state of confusion between useful and damaging. This type of confusion is another instance of the earlier mentioned "stowaways", the chunks of ignorance that get themselves stuck to good ideas. Non-selectivity and non-judgmentalness must not come at the cost of sound judgment and one's ability to discern. What, then, should these be like? Briefly, like this: non-selectivity in the course of listening to the other means non-reduction of the attentional field. If one's mind is sufficiently flexible and one is aware of the infinite-particulate-conditioned complexity of the flow of events, one will not presume to know what will later manifest as valuable. In the context of Vipassana meditation, as it is explained by S. N. Goenka, the meditator's attention should go on moving thoroughly and systematically across the entire field of sensations. Since she aims to achieve release from the habits of both aversion and attraction, she trains herself to be in motion: to feel each sensation, to pay attention to its characteristic changing, to avoid reacting with either desire or hatred, and to move on to the next area – no matter what sensation it might encounter there, no matter what the sensation that was left behind. In this sense it is a non-selective practice: she tries not to be tempted to dwell in one place or to escape another because of their inherent pleasure or displeasure, or due to some biased label stuck onto them by her mind's interpretive function. As concerns non-judgmentalness: In the therapeutic and interpersonal context it is a life-enabling mental position which gently holds experience without condemning it. In the space of meditation, non-judgmentalness is linked both to openness and to softness and compassion: The meditator does not judge a sensation as either good or bad but only sees that it is pleasant, neutral, or unpleasant, and that either way it is impermanent and essenceless and involves suffering. She does not judge the meditation hour she just finished as having been either good or bad, even though she recognizes that her mind was marked by more or less concentration, more or less equanimity, more or less right effort, awareness, or calm. She does not dignify her progress along the path as a great success or a blatant failure, understanding that the winding routes of life's events are endlessly complex, understanding that her responsibility is for her mental action and not for the fruit of that action, nor its pace and time of maturation, over which she has no control.

This is how the Buddha explains it: Just like the mason or his apprentice, when casting a look at the handle of the axe and observing the marks left by their hands, don't know: this much the handle was worn down today, this much yesterday, and even before. But they know all along that the handle is being worn down. In the same way, the meditator who is dedicated to practice doesn't know: this much craving and ignorance[8] were dissolved in me today, this much yesterday, and this much even before. And yet she knows and sees that they were dissolved and are still dissolving (AN 7.71). These are natural processes, and therefore they cannot be stopped or sped along. The hen's egg will hatch when the conditions have ripened, whether the hen craves it or not. The ropes of a boat will rot, wear away, and eventually disintegrate under the erosive forces of sun, water, and air. For the egg to hatch, the hen must continue brooding. For the boat's ropes to wear, they must be exposed for long enough to the forces of erosion. Then the chick will hatch, the ropes will crumble, ignorance and craving will dissolve, the chains of life and death disintegrate (AN 7.71).

It is an elusive way of perceiving reality. Elusive, but only until it becomes ingrained through long exposure to practice. It makes a distinction between the necessary participation of will and effort in the process of mental development and the involvement of desire and hatred which undermine that very development. Effort is indispensable for progress along the way and for learning from experience. It takes a systematic, ongoing effort to thwart the harmful habits of the mind which have been accumulating from times immemorial, and it takes a systematic, ongoing effort to develop what is advantageous. Effort, however, can be either right or an expression of violence, in which case it is aimed at achieving or getting rid of something on the assumption that one knows what's right and is in control of the results. To differentiate between these two requires close attention: the attention of a gentle mind, awake to the music of the processes, to being in and out of tune, to harmony and discord. This kind of attention is conscious of the quality of the effort and its sources: Here I find an effort arising in me that is based in a solid sense of self, in a grip on a hoped-for outcome, and in the need of that self to be absolved from the anxiety of unknowing. Here I find a proper effort, one associated with meticulous examination of the nature of my intention, of the mental activity itself, with the aspiration that it will be a pure mental action, without pretending to know where it will take me in the future and where it will lead me to strike local, temporary anchor. Meticulousness, in the spirit, is laid back. Attunement is loose. Wherever this is not the case, it may well be that the effort is of the first kind.

The non-instrumental approach, then, facilitates the balancing of effort. Altering the quality of attention, it changes from being a goading, searching, rushed, and scattered form of attention to an alert attention that leans back, ready to receive reality as it manifests itself. This thought puts us in mind of Freud's notion of the receptive organ; only this is already colored by a certain understanding of the intrapersonal and interpersonal dynamics of digestion and introjection, projection and transference – processes suggesting that the receptive organ also transmits, that between one organ and another (within the person and between her and another) there is constant communication flowing through different channels, and that it is our job to take cognizance of these channels and be open to them.

Rigidity, flexibility, and dissolution

We must therefore distinguish between the battle we should do and the non-violence with which we should do it. The battle is against the factors of suffering: ignorance, craving, and hatred. But precisely for this reason, it should be conducted non-violently; that is, employing an ethics of gentleness, which holds the components of experience tenderly. To tenderly hold experience as it is, a flexibility of mind is required. There tends to be an inverse relation between flexibility and anxiety: the more anxiety is active in the mind, wrapping itself around its very being, the more rigid the person becomes. He perceives and interprets reality through contact with his wounds – and this usually yields harsh sensations and correspondingly harsh reactions. When change comes his way, his mind reacts as though it were sandpaper against which the surroundings were rubbing, or like one who, in the face of danger, either pushes it away aggressively, or freezes on the spot, or withdraws, pained, into himself. Reality is painful: at times every aspect of it reaches us through a tissue of pain; and if the mind in such a condition has not meanwhile evolved the strength and ability to create space for breathing and clear observation (at the very time as the breath stalls; at the very time as pain throbs; at the very time anxiety shrouds) – then it shrinks and hardens, shutting down temporarily or cracking, growing somewhat brittle. How will it move along with change when it is in such a state? How will it ride the waves of experience?

I'm thinking of Balint's notion of the basic fault. When this is the region which we roam, whether on its margins – on the cusp of the abyss – or deep inside, then we must identify it. If the person I am with is the one acting from a wounded space, then I must understand that she cannot perceive the events clearly. I will say one thing, and she will hear another. I will make one gesture, and she will perceive another. Everything will slip down towards the abyss. Everything will hurt. When I am the one who is touched by reality in a rigid spot, a damaged layer not yet sufficiently healed, a zone perforated and cracked, I must understand that in such circumstances I cannot see reality properly. Obviously, I will only be able to realize this provided, over and beyond this zone, I also accommodate spacious and flexible ones. Space and flexibility enable inward reflection instead of denial, splitting, and projection. They allow contact with reality and learning, integration of experience, even when the reactions it arouses are harsh.

Reactions – the products of false perception and of past accumulations – entangle the components of experience that trigger them. They wrap themselves around them and exert pressure, creating a dark, dense region which signals anxiety and distress to other regions of the mind. Alternatively, they may not know what to do with the components of experience, passing them around like a hot potato, disgusted or panicked; or they kick them this way and that, hurling them at the mind's walls so they bounce back, and this leaves the mind eruptive, inflamed, spitting fire.

All this is called clinging. And as it loosens, as the reactions that produce it fade, unravel, and are uprooted, the mind grows stronger and more gentle, less violent, free to move with and linger with motion, attentive to reality, open to the air. And when the mind is in this state – flexible to the point of dissolution – mental materials simply pass through it. It's not that they are missed or disregarded, but that they are not captured in the mental space by reaction.

In terms of the Buddha's teaching, reactions are nothing but a varia-tion on the theme of craving and aversion. Misguided perception is what leads to them and again flows from their residues, and it can be called "delusion" or "ignorance" or "illusion". Clinging is entailed by reac-tions, and results in an incessant process of becoming. Together, these are the fuel of *saṃsāra*, the foundations of misery and violence. If we wish to eventually find a way out – while in the meantime gradually expanding our perspective and fostering a more flexible and dissolved attentional environment – we will have to act diligently against our bad habits and, at their expense, develop the beautiful qualities of the mind. This we may achieve by following the eightfold path, the path that leads to gentleness and to wisdom; we may, for this purpose, be helped by *ānāpāna*, the awareness of our natural breath as we focus on one small spot under the nose,[9] so that we may calm the mind, focus and sharpen it, control it enough so as to enable the next, main task. We may be helped by Vipassana, the penetrating insight achieved through systematic obser-vation of the entire field of sensations – an observation that requires movement – so as to practice awareness, equanimity, and non-clinging, and to undermine the roots of evil: ignorance, craving, and aversion.

Giving up on a sense of expertise

Contact with deep reality is impossible when the mind clings rigidly to its knowledge, when it fills itself or covers itself with a sense of exper-tise which removes it from things as they are. A sense of expertise is a sense of ownership over knowledge. Usually this amounts to a false type of solidifying, a way of achieving a good, organized, tightly held and soothing self-experience which, however, is anchored in illusion. It is the result of the mind's projective nature: its gap-filling nature, casting its desires, expectations, and memories onto reality; its denying, distorting, negating, and erasing nature, its creative and productive nature, which maintains the fragile illusion that we are prepared and therefore safe. We move about in the world with this projective mind, and we believe we are experts. Experts in what? Experts in life, our work, raising children; experts regarding ourselves, experts at reading and understanding people and situations. Surely, we can be skilled at some things: we may be deeply informed, highly experienced, conducting ourselves freely and elegantly in the field of our competence. But when we get set in our expert position and make it our state of mind or our attentional attitude, we will have produced conditions that are not open to reality, that attach it to a priori meanings which block it, conditions that shut the mind off to life.

Eigen wrote: "To learn from experience requires the tolerance of gaps that exert force on the field of meaning. Fertile meaning grows out of experience and gaps in experience and is not imposed in a disconnected way. One stays open to further nuances, shifts, corrections. More upheaval is always possible" (Eigen, 2004, Kindle location 1314–1316). This is the very essence of moving with experience and the experimental attitude (whether in the therapeutic setting or in everyday life), and it represents conditions that are the very opposite of the type of mental positions that forge something out of nothing or nullify what is, clogging the mind's arteries. As investigators, we are at our best when we are "whirling in mixed influences and slightly off balance (or, as it is called in science, capitalizing upon broken symmetry)" (Fleischman, 2013, p. 348), rather than when we believe we are experts. Whereas this is not always a comfortable or confidence-inspiring position, it is precisely the quality we must develop (or through which we must intermittently pass) if we wish to be in touch with reality as it arises. And so the position we should establish is a non-position: instead of a stationary solidity, attentive presence committed to moving along with the waves of experience.

A sense of expertise is associated with contraction around a defined self which presumes it knows some important facts. It sometimes happens that these facts grow out of all proportions, filling the entire field of knowing. Superficial confidence, in such a case, pushes out sincere exploration. Here a person is no longer in need of faith (F), nor is there a chance of her making contact with deeper realities (O). If she raises hypotheses, examines and investigates, the investigation in question is apparent only. The evidence she encounters will not always be allowed entry in the domain of her saturated knowledge. It will bounce and ricochet against its hard walls, or else it may reorganize in order to confirm what was already solid. Every fact has value depending on the context in which it appears; when this context is removed and replaced by another (through a disconnected etiology; through a suffocating causality; through an imposed interpretation), the fact turns into a distorted piece of reality which the mind uses for its own purposes. Ignoring facts is self-deception, but close adherence to facts as such stifles the non-intellectual part of the mind,[10] the most fertile ground of hypotheses. And so we must combine an intelligent and probing skepticism, seeking adequate evidence for our assumptions, together with wonder: the willingness to not close down and obstruct (Fleischman, 2013). "We have to be prepared to both reject and accept. People who wonder do not hold on tight. There are both errors and revelations in both dismissals and beliefs. We need to be skeptical, flexible, and ready for more" (Fleischman, 2013, p. 331).

The world expands and dissolves before our very eyes, each and every moment. Especially these days, in a reality of accelerated change, a reality where the overflow of communication keeps exposing this change and holding out its expressions – how can we think of ourselves as experts? We may be experts regarding certain niches of the universe, tentative local experts; but experts of the inner universe, experts of the external universe – unless we reach the highest degrees of liberation (which is a rare achievement) – this we cannot claim to be. Taken from this perspective, it is our job – teachers, therapists, parents, friends, explorers of the mind, meditators, people in the world – to undercut instrumental thinking, to abandon the position of expertise and to move from rigidity to flexibility, and from flexibility to dissolution. This role is most valuable, but it is also weightless: it is light and ethereal, present only to be shed, shed only to be further elaborated and to act. At times this role has to harden and take on form, but only in response to a situation that requires it. Otherwise, and even when it seems to have become firm, it should not consolidate into a persona, into a cover of selfhood put on to achieve a sense of solidity in an evolving and transient world, to cling to a knowledge that naturally slips away as soon as one takes hold of it.

From chaos, form arises

A non-clinging mind can be alert when the selected fact (Bion, 1962) arises – the fact that transforms the muddled mess into something coherent, which casts a new light on what hitherto seemed inconceivable, meaningless, disconnected. If the mind of that moment is clear and free of craving, it will be able to make an attuned use of the selected fact: one that joins the frequency of the current processes that form as it looks on, momentarily seeming to solidify in order then to shed their shape, drop into the abyss, wither away.

Well-attuned use of the selected fact requires a type of attention marked by balanced precision. This quality relies on identifying the movement that links the ancient past of the inner and outer universe with present events of body and mind, which are actually the former's manifestations; a movement which expands continuously into the future, one that emerges in the course of action, before our curious and perplexed eyes, from under our comforting, soothing hands, or way out behind the scenes, beyond our limited capacities to sense, to metabolize, to perceive.

Reality reveals itself moment by moment on a wealth of strata, in an infinity of details. Communication and information flow fast, either hitting or not hitting receptors, then to be processed by self-parts which one way or another attach interpretations to them. And we try to loosen our grip and stay in touch (with the other, with experience). We try to follow the motion. This moving along with experience often has a quality of lingering; but being nevertheless marked by an oscillation, it belongs in the realm of change and motion. Still, paradoxically, the mind that is most open to movement also includes a part that tends to zero movement. Zero movement, in this context, is *upekkhā*: the mental quality that is neither repelled nor attracted.

If it is open to change and movement, if it is neither repelled nor attracted (or, alternatively, it repels but another part of the mind notices this and examines the repulsion; it is attracted but another part of the mind notices this and examines the attraction) – then it needs not know in advance and thus shut itself off from knowing. Subsequently it surrenders to events, allowing coherence to emerge from chaos by itself.

Coherence is not solidity either, and it has no fixed identity. Coherence is, perhaps, directionality: a fluctuating directionality, that of the flow of components, processes, combinations, and relations which pours through time and space, responding to a multitude of systems that constrain and channel it but also leave it much space for variation, for an unexpected creativity (Fleischman, 2013). Often, what keeps coherence hidden, what confounds us, is an apparent contradiction. Infantile strata, of the kind that Klein described so well, stay with us and may pop up at the most unlikely places. Like the infant, who, in his immaturity, facing an all-too-complex reality (complex reality meeting simple equipment), uses a strategy of splitting, so are we: having to deal with a hyper-complex reality, whose infinite temporality and spatiality we are unable to grasp; whose winding causality we cannot follow; the speed of change of whose particles, if we were to acknowledge it, would spell the dissolution of our sense of solidity – we, too, form dichotomies and project them onto reality. We imagine that reality may be either certain or uncertain, personal or universal, ongoing or transient; that it might be driven either by a strict determinism or by free will, by capricious accident or by a creator with a blueprint and a purpose (Fleischman, 2013). All these notions, however, are nothing but ways of reorganizing a complex world within a narrow, anxious mind. Under their influence we experience the world one-dimensionally or two-dimensionally and find it hard to figure how certain elements in it can coexist with others. Confusion is unpleasant, and the sense of contradiction, too, makes us feel uncomfortable. And so we attempt to settle them forcefully and with a conviction that ousts reality. A good attentional environment involves the ability to distinguish the various layers of reality, the features of its specific phenomena, and the specific relations they entertain. It is a mental space ridded of subjugation to the illusive dichotomies the mind usually tends to produce and project onto the world. Paradox exists, opposing forces exist; not all ways lead to Rome. The sense of contradiction, however, is merely an expression of our embattled ego, evidence of our hazy mental condition.

A realistic mind is not confused by a sense of contradiction. It offers living space to the components of experience, space to be and to unfold at their natural pace. It makes no effort to manipulate them, spur them to vanish or to consolidate or to undergo any other type of change it believes they should undergo. A mind like this – even if it is still weighed down by residues of ignorance and suffering – has cultivated a part situated beyond considerations of utility and therefore beyond conflict. It is able to feel the components of experience simultaneously, without forcing one component to exclude another, oppose it, vanquish it or be subdued by it. It can hold together pain and beauty, fragility and might, shame alongside the part that is eager to forge ahead at full speed, great terror alongside the universal envelope, existent and non-existent, manifesting and fading away, pulling strings of safety unanchored in firm ground.

Coherence and infinite complexity, like many other pairs the mind tends to keep apart, do not clash (Fleischman, 2013). Coherence is the product of a clarification resulting from non-clinging observation of the world of phenomena – a multi-dimensional observation that touches several levels of reality at once. A mind that perceives this can feel at ease in constant flux without having a need to know the end in advance. At times this ease is accompanied by pleasantness; at other times it is a subterranean layer underneath distress, fear, disturbing presence. The more sensitive to truth the mind becomes, wide open before it, trembling with all these yet not collapsing – the better able it is to act non-violently towards reality, towards others, towards itself. This is the privilege, the opportunity, the responsibility of being a sensitive being in the world. This is the privilege, the opportunity, the responsibility of being human.

Conditioned arising: an environment within the self within the environment

Environment is the material context, the characteristics of our physical habitat, but also the mental context and sphere of living. Given that there are six sensory fields – the five customarily mentioned in the west, plus the sixth one, that of the mind – then, much like the eye encounters shapes and colors, the mind encounters mental objects: images, ideas, emotional contents, memories, thoughts. In the Buddhist perspective, everything that receives is "internal", and any object that makes contact with whatever receives is "external". If this is so, then the thought that comes to mind is no less extraneous to me than the sound of the wind reaching my ears.

Thought is extraneous. Feeling is extraneous. Anxiety is not me. Doubt is not me. But nor is the mind – the receptive organ, considered "internal". Nevertheless, it is my full responsibility to cope with the contents of this mind: with thought, feeling, anxiety, and doubt. I am responsible for cultivating this mind so it will be able to handle them well, so it will be a good attentional environment. I alone will bear the consequences of my mental reaction to experience. Exactly whose responsibility is it to cope and to cultivate, if mental contents are not mine, if the mind is not mine? Who will bear the consequences if all these are neither me nor mine? The answer is set forth in the law of *kamma* and in the principle of conditioned arising: Every mental act has its own outcome, even if the one who bears it is nothing but a formation of a current, a singular though transient manifestation devoid of a self-core.

And to return to the inter-psychic environment: Much like the quality of the air affects me – the air I breathe, which enters my lungs and touches my skin – so do the qualities of the mental materials surrounding me, those that others produce and spread around. Though these materials are extraneous to me, they touch me. The consciousness of my mind-sense picks them up, my *saññā* labels and interprets them on the basis of past experience; they give rise to physical sensations to which my *saṅkhāra* reacts this way or that, or not at all. These materials are external to me, but not all that much more external than my own thoughts, with which I'm more likely to identify. The thoughts and feelings triggered in me arise as a result of a cluster of events: of the combination of present impressions that touch my mind-body system and the reactive residues they evoke. The mental materials circulating in my surroundings, offspring of the frenzied brains of those who are with me, also join the ensemble of conditions, internal and external, that form the complex of events producing additional mental materials in me.

Some thoughts are in search of a thinker, said Bion. A thought, obviously, is not an essential entity which exits the mind that conceived it to make its way to the entrance of another mind. But the mental materials accompanying this thought or arousing it can most definitely move along, pass through the inter-psychic space, make contact with another mind, then either arouse or not arouse correlated or complementary experiences and thoughts. Coming in from this direction or coming in from another, they all touch us; all are objects. They all are potentially stimulating; not one of them personal, but we personally experience them.

It is helpful to notice the chain of events: what led up to what, and what arrived from where. Though the chain of events is both infinite and multi-dimensional, sufficient experience and clarity of mind enable us to pinpoint segments of it: what object the gates of my senses encountered, what consciousness registered, how the perceptive function interpreted it, what sensations arose as a result, and what reactions these triggered, if any. Noticing this contributes to the investigation of phenomena conducted by the researcher of the mind on an experiential basis, and when the conditions are right, it aids a clear understanding of reality. At the end of the day, however, no matter what the course of events, one's attitude should be the same: an object of the senses is an object of the senses. The sensation brought about by the object's contact with its respective sensory gate is a sensation. And it is the mind's reactivity (or non-reactivity) that determines the outcomes of the event for that particular mind, as well as the nature of the mental materials it puts back into the interpersonal space, its surroundings.

Here are some classic questions: How do I know what's mine and what's hers? How do I know that what I seem to observe in him is not merely my projection? How do I know if what I feel right now was expelled from the mind of the person in front of me, or rather something I brought in from home?

All of these are important, largely ethical questions. And they are associated with the (intuitive, normative) confusion regarding conceptions of inside and outside, the nature of the dividing lines between these, and the very value of this division. However, when "internal" is everything that takes in (the eye consciousness, the ear consciousness, the olfactory consciousness, the taste consciousness, the tactile consciousness, and the mind consciousness) and "external" is every object taken in (the sound of the words of the person in front of me, for instance; his facial expression, as well as the thought that passes through my mind as I hear his words and see his face) – then the status of these questions changes. Then our focus of attention shifts away from the field of thought, impelled by the need to make the distinction between self and non-self, between mine and not-mine – towards the field of thought dedicated to the distinction between dull and calibrated, between non-beneficial and beneficial, between reactive and balanced. On the basis of these distinctions, one can conduct oneself: Wherever I recognize that my state of mind is non-instrumental, fairly calibrated, attuned and flexible, I assume that the materials passing through my system, my alpha function, my *reverie*, are useful substances which can serve well the process and its participants. The dualism between inside and outside, between self and non-self, is suspended under these circumstances. It isn't that we simply become one. We don't fuse. But our encounter permeates space, occupying a considerable part of our being. The channel of unconscious communication between us is unobstructed and communication flows freely (at least in one direction). Similarly, the duality between conscious and unconscious dissipates in me for a while, and the channel of communication between the conscious and unconscious levels of processing opens. Information flows through it – from O to K – unobstructed.

At other times, when I recognize that my mind is dull or scattered, reactive or restless, I know that I must relate slightly differently to the emergent materials. Then the inside-outside dialectic changes, requiring a more cautious examination of the contents formulated or otherwise represented in the interpersonal space. This is not to say, of course, that there is no room for them: as the in-depth discussion of projective identification and countertransference has shown, the therapist's reactive attentional-perceptual-emotional states – conditions that involve confusion and suffering – can become valuable provided they are accompanied by awareness and a sufficient digestive ability. We are creatures with subjective, biased minds trying to examine reality without being blind to the bias we impose on it. It is, however, exactly this that returns us to our unique position: that of those whose solution to the mystery of their suffering and release inheres in the exploration of the universe. Of those for whom there is no full exploration of the universe without exploration of themselves. Of those who must struggle against their inner violence without reaching for violence, paving their way between the forces of illusion and destruction with nothing but the pure equipment of gentleness in their hands.

Notes

1   The mind's reactive function, the mental intention or action (which is also *kamma*, or in Sanskrit: *karma*). Basically, *saṅkhāra* is the movement towards the pleasant and away from the unpleasant, which very rapidly evolves into thirst; i.e., into craving or aversion. As such, it is considered (together with thirst and clinging) the fuel that keeps the cycle of becoming and suffering going. Both the creating factor and the thing created are embodied in the term *saṅkhāra*: both the mental action that produces patterns and habits, as well as the patterns and habits themselves, which prompt new action. It is one of the five aggregates that constitute the phenomenon we call "self": *viññāṇa*, *saññā*, *vedanā*, *saṅkhāra*, and *rūpa* – consciousness, perception, sensation, reaction, and form or matter, i.e., the body, the corporeal aspect.

2 The mind's perceptual, conceptual, interpretive, evaluating function. Its categorizations and evaluations are based on earlier experiences with objects it identifies as similar.
3 Virtuous friends, companions, and colleagues (*kalyāṇamitta, kalāyāṇasahāya, kalāyāṇasampavaṅka*): they are moral, honest, pure, learned, and wise companions (Rhys Davids & Stede, 1921–1925) who wish for the person's wellbeing and his progress on the path (Nyanatiloka, 1997). The ultimate "good friend" is the Buddha (ibid.).
4 This list is not a word-by-word translation; it is in part a summary.
5 Transformation Tα →Tβ of preverbal material.
6 The limbic system is a set of brain structures (not an independent system) which is central to emotional experience and memory.
7 The authors mention this is based on: Bion, Wilfred R. 1976. "Four discussions." In: *Clinical Seminars and Other Works*, 241–292. London: Karnac, 1994.
8 Taints, corruptions, intoxicates, biases or *āsava*, in the Pāli original; lit. secretion, influx and outflux. The four *āsavas* are those of sensual desires, of the craving for existence, of ignorance, and of wrong views.
9 Different teachers suggest different spots to focus on when practicing *ānāpāna*.
10 Fleischman calls this simply "the heart".

Reference

Aharoni, H. & Bergstein, A. (2012). Annotated translation and other papers of W. R. Bion, *Caesura*. Tel Aviv: Bookworm.
AN 6.55.
AN 7.71.
Barnea-Astrog, M. (2015). Internal holding, external holding: three experiences in primitive fear of annihilation. *Hebrew Psychology*. Accessed May 18, 2015 at: www.hebpsy.net/articles.asp?id=3252.
Barnea-Astrog, M. (2017). *Carved by Experience: Vipassana, Psychoanalysis, and the Mind Investigating Itself*. London: Karnac.
Besnard, A., Caboche, J. & Laroache, S. (2012). Reconsolidation of memory: a decade of debate. *Progress in Neurobiology*, 99 (1): 61–80.
Bion, W. R. (1962). *Learning from Experience*. London: Tavistock.
Bion, W. R. (1970). *Attention and Interpretation*. London: Tavistock.
DN 27.
Eigen, M. (2004). *Psychic Deadness*. London: Karnac.
Fleischman, P. R. (2013). *Wonder: When and Why the World Appears Radiant*. Amherst: Small Batch Books.
Freud, S. (1911). Formulations on the two principles of mental functioning. *S.E.*, *12*: 213–226.
Goenka, S. N. (2006). *The Gem Set in Gold*. Igatpuri: Vipassana Research Institute.
Grotstein, J. S. (1995). Projective identification reappraised – projective identification, introjective identification, the transference/countertransference neurosis/

psychosis, and their consummate expression in the crucifixion, the Pietà, and "Therapeutic Exorcism," Part II: The countertransference complex. *Contemporary Psychoanalysis, 31*: 479–520.

Hupbach, A., Gomez, R., Hardt, O. & Nadel, L. (2007). Reconsolidation of episodic memories: a subtle reminder triggers integration of new information. *Learning & Memory, 14* (1–2): 47–53.

Nothnagel, K. (2015). A translation of Upaḍḍhasuttaṃ (SN 45.2), lesson 3.1.8. *Exploring the path, online Pāli program.* Accessed June 16, 2018 at: learning. pariyatti.org/mod/page/view.php?id=368.

Nyanatiloka (1997). *Buddhist Dictionary: Manual of Buddhist Terms and Doctrines* (4th revised ed.). Edited by Nyanaponika. Kandy, Sri Lanka: Buddhist Publication Society.

Przybyslawski, J. & Sara, S. J. (1997). Reconsolidation of memory after its reactivation. *Behavioral Brain Research, 84* (1–2): 241–246.

Rhys Davids, T. W., & Stede, W. (Eds.) (1921–1925). *The Pāli Text Society's Pāli–English Dictionary.* Chipstead: Pāli Text Society.

SN 45.2.

Snp 2.4.

Symington, J. (1985). The survival function of primitive omnipotence. *International Journal of Psycho-Analysis, 66*: 481–487.

Thanissaro Bhikkhu (2006). Notes on Ambalatthika-Rahulovada Sutta: Instructions to Rahula at Mango Stone (MN 61). *Access to Insight.* Accessed December 21, 2016 at: www.accesstoinsight.org/tipitaka/mn/mn.061.than.html.

Winnicott, D. W. (1971). Mirror-role of mother and family in child development. In: *Playing and Reality* (pp. 111–118). London: Tavistock.

Epilogue
Reflections on time and space

We undertake the difficult task of investigating reality by means of a tool that is in the grip of blindness – a blindness that is itself an expression of present reality. How are we to be at peace in such an unsettling state? How are we to have full faith in a condition which is inextricably entangled with doubt? To a great extent, this is what F in O means. The instrumental attitude leads us to judge events as positive or negative according to the inner and outer environment's reactions to them. Desirable events are related to pleasantness; undesirable ones to unpleasantness. This is our habit, the default option, and usually we don't take further, more thorough notice of it. But if we judge things by a more profound criterion – this is not the measure we would use.

Our limited sensory and mental equipment does not allow us to attain comprehensive certainty. It is difficult to follow the complex, beginningless routes of causality. How exactly did these different factors join to lead up to this moment? Where will the next action take us? We have no way of knowing this, but we do have the capacity to make out certain features of the processes, to trace the general outlines of the regularity guiding them and to understand the basic direction into which it points. In the words of the Buddha: we are unable, in our limited state, to follow the vicissitudes of action (*kamma*) and its fruit (*phala*), but we can see that action free of ignorance, craving, and aversion will take us on the path of liberty, while action afflicted by these will drag us further down the crevices of reaction, along the slopes of repetition, to the swamps of confusion and illusion.

A realistic and penetrating look at infinite complexity and its specific expressions stirs wonder in the mind, a sense of responsibility, modesty, and gratitude. We can definitely know; however, we must be able to see what kind of knowing it is. Is it knowing of the relative and the subjective? Of the universal and objective? Is this the knowing of the absolute?

Identifying a temporary phenomenon is not the same as identifying the temporality of phenomena, and both of these are unlike attaining what is beyond time and phenomenality. Each of these mental events has its own status, and penetrating sight occurs whenever it is possible to distinguish between them. Such a view will include at least the two first events (the third is not easily achieved or experienced. To be precise, it cannot in fact be called an "event" or "mental", and we cannot even really claim it is somewhere out there to be reached). As we differentiate the various levels of reality and the knowledge of reality, we should also identify the web of connections between them. We should see that the external world is revealed in the internal world, and the internal world in the external; that the mental is revealed in the material and the material is revealed in the mental, and that the universal manifests itself in the relative-subjective. We may go on splitting ourselves along the imaginary seam between inside and outside, between subjective and objective, between self and non-self. We may go on being torn by the conflicts this imaginary line produces, and like blind people, feel our ways through the mists of perplexity it spreads. Yet we can also shed all these, penetrate the illusions of dualism and fusion, and see reality: "Creation and destruction are continuities, and we ourselves are glowing with energy waves from the nuclear lights. Starlight continues to glow inside us. We not only find stars beautiful, haunting, and inspiring, but we are their offspring. We are transient children of bigger impermanence" (Fleischman, 2013, p. 334).

We observe the waves of experience in their motion: the arising and decay of the inner and outer universe, solidification and dissolution, extinction and growth. We are living beings, and living beings are sensing beings. If goodness has come our way, we are aware of our sensations. If goodness has come our way, we are gentle towards them, treat them softly, try to be less reactive. If goodness has come our way, we see that this splendor whose children we are reveals itself to us. It radiates from the face of the person in front of us, from our own minds, from the web of body-mind relations that arises between us. The realistic, penetrating, multi-dimensional gaze, beholden to reality, does not settle for superficial reality. Looking at it, it looks through it. It is open to discovery, to subtlety, to splendor, to uncertainty. It holds gentleness tenderly.

And tenderness is required. And along with it, patience, discernment, faith sheltered by truth, perseverance in cultivating non-clinging and awareness. Because the processes involved are complex, hyper-complex, quantum-complex. We don't know at what stage of maturity they are at any given moment, at what point (a multi-dimensional point, a channel, a wormhole) we enter and join them, and how we are affected by them and affect them in return. The processes we make out are usually no more than local segments.

Local segments. Bits of events. Shreds of fluid, ephemeral time and space. Shreds of time and space that, as they pass through our limited minds, get caught like on a hook. Like in a sticky net. They get stuck and congeal.

The present moment's blend of circumstances is a local segment. The string of events that led me to this life event or another is a local segment too. All of my life: a local segment. What does this say about the present moment? What does it say about me?

Sometimes, sitting in the midst of my sense of self, I quietly wonder when it will cease. When the muscles of attention will loosen, when the container will be left in peace and only the contained remain, when the holder will be dropped and only the held remain. In the seen – only the seen. In the heard – only the heard. In the felt – only the felt. In the cognized – only the cognized (Ud 1.10). Mere knowing along with mere awareness (DN 22), without a self to interfere (Ud 1.10).

For Winnicott, it is only understandable that someone who was not fortunate enough to receive proper holding early on in life will have to make an effort to create a holding envelope for himself. Having no choice but to focus on this outer layer, his core will suffer neglect. The past is now history, and the residues of events have crumbled in part while others remain active. I'm sitting in my sense of self, in an envelope that tries hard to generate itself, at least for now, as if forever. I look inside: at the envelope, at the so-called "core"; I cast about in the container and sift its contents. Not too bad, the work this container does. Not too awful, the materials it has to process. Not too false, this core. Yet, even if the core is not neglected, even if the self is "true" – it is nevertheless false. I am, nevertheless, held in an envelope, preoccupied by the shell. Because the core is a shell too.

Investing in formative processes, focusing on the operations of the envelope and the container, are suffused with discontent by nature. A similar fate, however, awaits adherence to contents. Freedom arises from non-clinging. From "moving with", which is the result of non-movement, from the possibility to join attention to its object of observation with a dissolved stability, with a non-solid firmness.

The new chick will emerge from the egg when it is time for him to emerge. The boat's ropes will tear when they're worn down. The fruit will ripen when the season comes. The responsibility is entirely mine to create the conditions for emergence, for erosion, for ripening. Vacant are my hands of the equipment of certainty, the illusion of omnipotence and control.

I float in my sense of self and facing me is another person, caught up in his own shell and core. I see him and he sees me – the gates of our senses meet. Through my eyes and my skin I extend my hand to him. A metaphoric hand, a spring of good will. In this very moment, others are doing exactly the same as me: in rooms, in offices, outdoors. Because suffering is real and we really want to help. But the processes before us are complicated, quantum-complicated, hyper-complicated. We don't know at which stage of maturity they are at any given moment, at what point (a multi-dimensional point, a channel, a wormhole) we enter and join them, nor how we affect and in turn are affected by them.

As the mind grows subtle, this complexity becomes clear, unravels itself. Dimensions upon dimensions, layers upon layers of microscopic mind-and-matter processes unfold, teeming inside and around us. As the mind grows subtle, humility arises in their presence as well as wonder, and the wish to sow seeds of goodness at every moment of awareness, equanimity, and compassion that makes it possible – positive particles, light touches whose ripples send tiny waves of purity to others' infinite shores of suffering. As the mind grows subtle, recognition arises that it is our mental state, our mental contents and actions, that contrive all this. That mind precedes all phenomena, that it produces them (Dhp 1–2). That if we try to help while our mind is troubled, blind to subterranean goings-on, or in thrall to an instrumental position which adheres to outcomes, we will not be very useful, if at all. That when our mind is free of lust, tender, stable as it trembles with the other's heart – then our contribution to the situation will be the best we can possibly make, and we can let go of the need to know the results.

Still, we are blindfolded, perceiving reality through the particular filters of our particular self. Still, we are shrouded in transference projections, casting the contents of our minds onto reality, taking it back in stained, reacting to it through old frames. Still, we crave and hate, pursue pleasure and try hard to avoid pain, insensate and lazy or restless and anxious, consumed by doubt about others or the world or ourselves. But the more these subside, the more infrequent they become, suspended briefly or even gone – the better we can see.

Endless complexity. Suffering. The waves of clarity that rise in us and come forth. The changing face of the other, as their ripples touch the shores of his suffering. Our own face changing
As waves rise
Touch
Return to shore.

***

References

Dhp 1–2.
DN 22.
Fleischman, P. R. (2013). *Wonder: When and Why the World Appears Radiant.* Amherst: Small Batch Books.
Ud 1.10.

Index

accuracy 50, 54, 117–118
aesthetics 2, 115
alpha elements 82
alpha function 32, 45, 82, 141
Alvarez, A. 44–45, 55–56
anatman (*anattā*) 105n2
annihilation 4, 24, 77, 81; and pain
  and pleasure 42, 46, 54, 65
arising 30, 62, 69n6; and attention as
  an environment 117, 130, 133, 146;
  and being at home 73, 77, 84, 86,
  88, 95, 104; conditioned 108–112,
  139–142
āsava 143n8
associating 112–113
attention 4, 6, 14, 147; and accuracy
  117–118; and associating
  112–113; and being at home 73,
  75, 79–80, 87–88, 90–94, 96; case
  study relevant to 122–127; and
  conditioned arising 139–142; and
  discord and harmony 115–117;
  as an environment 108; and
  environmental toxicity 114; and
  expertise 135–137; and form
  137–139; and holding and letting
  go 127–129; and the interpersonal
  120–122; and the mental space
  118–120; and movement 129–13;
  and non-violence 133–135; and
  pain and pleasure 45, 53–54;
  and the path of gentleness 20,
  26, 31–35; and self-environment
  relations 108–112; and thinking
  130–133

awareness 6, 13–14, 124; and
  accuracy 117; of *anatman* 105n2;
  and being at home 81–82, 85,
  87–88, 93–94; and conditioned
  arising 142; and expertise 135;
  and letting go 128; and pain and
  pleasure 66–68; and the path of
  gentleness 16, 20–22, 26, 31–32,
  34; right awareness 37n1, 70n8;
  and self-environment relations
  110, 112; and thinking 132; and
  time and space 146–148; *see also*
  mindfulness

babies *see* infants
Balint, M. 47–48, 121, 134
becoming 3; and attention as an
  environment 108, 120, 135; and
  being at home 75, 82, 86, 96; and
  fear 76–81; and pain and pleasure
  40, 48, 60, 62, 64, 70n7; and the
  path of gentleness 21, 24, 29,
  35; *saṅkhāra* and 142n1;
  un-becoming 74
behavior 4; and attention as an
  environment 110, 113, 128; and
  being at home 87, 92, 94–96;
  and pain and pleasure 41, 61, 64;
  and the path of gentleness 17–21,
  26–30, 34; *samādhi* and 70n8
beta elements 128
big bang 77–81
Bion, W. R.: and attention as an
  environment 118, 121, 140; and
  being at home 75; and fear 77–78;

115, 117, 123–124, 131; and being
at home 102; and pain and pleasure
40, 45, 50, 53; and the path of
gentleness 19, 22, 26, 30; subtle
pleasantness 66–69
surrender 47, 52, 86–87, 90, 97,
99–100; holding and 90–96
Suskind, P. *Perfume* 10–11

taṇhā 24, 60, 69n6
terror *see* fear
thinking 33; and attention as an
environment 113, 119; and being at
home 77, 82; instrumental vs. non-
instrumental 130–133, 137; and
pain and pleasure 42, 44, 55, 64
thirst 24, 64–65, 69, 142n1; sensation
and 59–60; *see also taṇhā*
time 3, 48, 56, 63, 77, 79–81, 138,
145–149
tone 8–9, 50–51, 117
toxicity 27, 32, 114, 116–117
transference 133, 148; *see also*
countertransference
transformation 69n3, 82–83, 97, 102,
109, 119
truth 6, 13, 146; and attention as an
environment 108, 115, 117, 119,
139; and being at home 74–75,
78, 89, 94–100, 104, 105n2;
and the interpersonal attentional
environment 120–122; and pain
and pleasure 43, 55–56, 58, 62, 66,

70n8; and the path of gentleness
16, 32–33; reflections on the
attitude to 35–37; and the signs of
existence 82–86; truth principle
42; *see also* four noble truths

unpleasantness 53, 58, 60–61, 65, 73,
103, 119
unpleasure 65
upādāna 69n6, 96
upekkhā (mental equilibrium) 70n8,
122, 138

violence 11; and attention as an
environment 116, 125, 133, 135,
142; and being at home 75, 85–86,
99; and the path of gentleness 19,
23–24, 30, 37
Vipassana (Vipassanā) 7, 57, 66; and
attention as an environment 131,
135; and pain and pleasure 76, 93;
and the path of gentleness 16–17,
21, 26–27

Winnicott, D. W. 6, 12, 32–33,
74–75, 120–121, 147; and pain
and pleasure 45–48, 54
wisdom 122, 124, 135; and being at
home 87–88, 90, 93; and beings in
higher realms 69n2; the eightfold
path and 37n1; meditation and
17–21; and pain and pleasure
51–52, 58